· VOICES ·
from
COLONIAL AMERICA

TEXAS

1527 – 1836

MICHAEL TEITELBAUM

WITH

ANDRÉS RESÉNDEZ, PH.D., CONSULTANT

NATIONAL GEOGRAPHIC

WASHINGTON, D.C.

STAFF FOR THIS BOOK

Nancy Laties Feresten, *Vice President, Editor-in-Chief*
  of Children's Books
Suzanne Patrick Fonda, *Project Editor*
Robert D. Johnston, Ph.D., *Associate Professor and Director,*
  Teaching of History Program University of Illinois at Chicago,
  Overall Series Editor
Bea Jackson, *Design Director, Children's Books and Education*
  Publishing Group
Jean Cantu, *Illustrations Specialist*
Carl Mehler, *Director of Maps*
Justin Morrill, *The M Factory, Inc., Map Research,*
  Design, and Production
Jen Agresta, *Indexer*
Rebecca Hinds, *Managing Editor*
R. Gary Colbert, *Production Director*
Lewis R. Bassford, *Production Manager*
Vincent P. Ryan and Maryclare Tracy, *Manufacturing Managers*

Voices from Colonial Texas was prepared by
CREATIVE MEDIA APPLICATIONS, INC.

Michael Teitelbaum, *Writer*
Fabia Wargin Design, Inc., *Design and Production*
Matt Levine, *Editor*
Susan Madoff, *Associate Editor*
Laurie Lieb, *Copyeditor*
Jennifer Bright, *Image Researcher*
Lauren Thogersen, *Content Researcher*

Body text is set in Deepdene, sidebars are Caslon 337 Oldstyle, and display text is Cochin Archaic Bold.

LIBRARY OF CONGRESS CATALOGING-IN-PUBLICATION DATA
Teitelbaum, Michael.
  Voices from colonial America. Texas, 1527–1836 / by Michael Teitelbaum.
    p. cm. — (Voices from colonial America)
  Includes bibliographical references and index.
  ISBN 0–7922–6387-1 (Hardcover)
  ISBN 0–7922–6682-x (Library)
1. Texas—History—To 1846—Juvenile literature. I. Title: Texas, 1527–1836. II. Title. III. Series.
  F389.T36 2005
  976.4'01—dc22
                                        2005011450
Printed in Belgium

CONTENTS

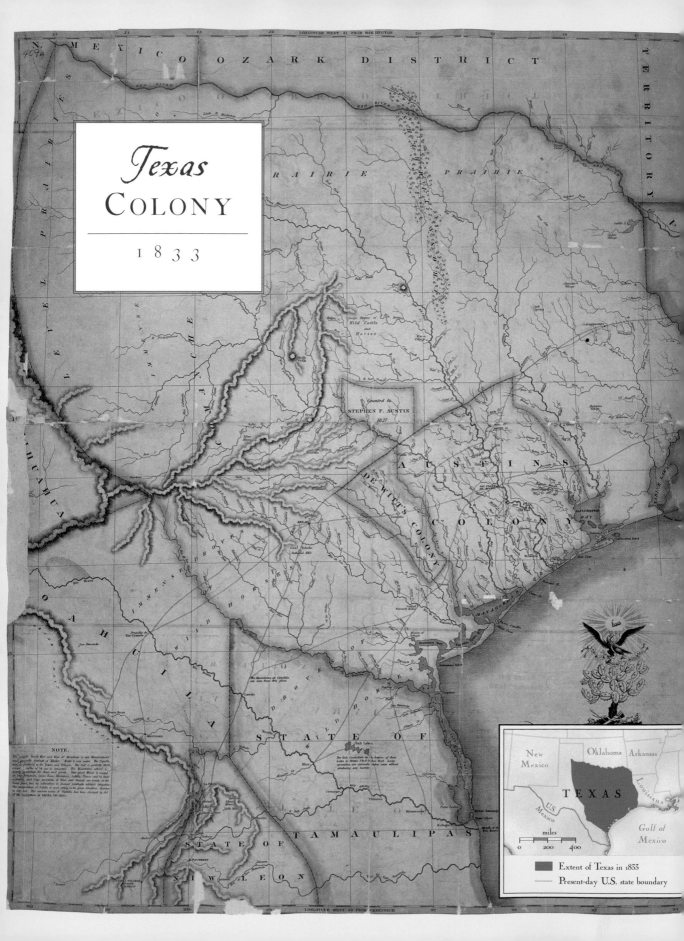

Texas
COLONY
1 8 3 3

Extent of Texas in 1833

Present-day U.S. state boundary

INTRODUCTION

by

Andrés Reséndez, Ph.D.

The Texas cattle drive became a part of the folklore and legend of Texas
as a state full of cowboys and wide-open spaces.

In September 1960 John Steinbeck, the famous author from
California and soon to be Nobel-prize winner, loaded his
bags on a double-doored rattler and together with his poodle
began speeding across America to get reacquainted with this
enormous land that he had spent his entire life writing about.
He dreaded grappling with the self-confident state of Texas,

OPPOSITE: This map shows the area of Texas a few years before it won its
independence from Mexico. It includes the boundaries of some American
settlements called empresarios, roadways, villages and missions, rivers and
other physical features, and regions where herds of wild horses roam.

but he could not escape it. "*I could have bypassed Texas about as easily as a space traveler can avoid the Milky Way. It sticks its big old Panhandle up north and it slops and slouches along the Rio Grande. Once you are in Texas it seems to take forever to get out, and some people never make it.*" Steinbeck rightfully observed that Texas, "*like most passionate nations, has its own private history, based on, but not limited by, facts.*" He also noted that contemporary Texans like to nurture the tradition of the frontier cattleman with boots and ranches and all.

Texas is a gigantic state inhabited by many peoples. It possesses a long history that stretches well before the Alamo and the cattle runs. To immerse oneself in this history is to discover different groups of Indians living in a world of their own so vastly different from today's that we can only begin to imagine it. It is to follow pioneering Spanish and French explorers, missionaries, and entrepreneurs struggling to establish footholds in this harsh environment and seeking to compete against one another and dominate the natives. It is to learn about unique institutions like missions and presidios, so thoroughly European in inspiration and yet so well adapted to the demands of the New World. Finally, it is to understand the tumultuous process through which an enormous territory internally divided became a Spanish province and then a Mexican state which, in turn, would become an independent republic and finally an American state.

Voices from Colonial America: Texas will introduce young readers to this rich microcosm of peoples, events, and ideas that have contributed so much to make Texas what it is today.

OPPOSITE: The independent Republic of Texas issued its first paper money in 1837. In 1838, Texas issued bills with decorative designs and portraits of notable Texans, including Stephen Austin on the fifty dollar bill.

Spanish Arrival in Texas

CABEZA DE VACA OF SPAIN *washes up on the shores of Texas.*
After living with the Indians for eight years, he arrives in
Mexico City and reports that the area is not worth colonizing.

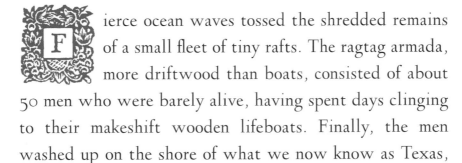

ierce ocean waves tossed the shredded remains of a small fleet of tiny rafts. The ragtag armada, more driftwood than boats, consisted of about 50 men who were barely alive, having spent days clinging to their makeshift wooden lifeboats. Finally, the men washed up on the shore of what we now know as Texas, near modern-day Galveston.

Álvar Núñez Cabeza de Vaca of Spain and his comrades became the first Europeans to set foot in what would

OPPOSITE: Álvar Núñez Cabeza de Vaca and his men washed ashore at present-day Galveston, Texas, in 1528, after a month at sea fighting for their lives aboard makeshift rafts.

become the 28th state of the United States. The year was 1528. Who were these men, and how did they happen to arrive on the shore of Texas?

Beginning in the late 1400s, Spain sought to expand its power and territory into the New World (as Europeans called the Americas). The Spanish also believed in legends of cities brimming with treasure, there for the taking in the newly discovered lands. With these motivations, Spanish explorers and conquistadores began their conquest.

conquistadores— Spanish soldiers who defeated the Indians of Mexico and other places in the Americas

Spain's desire to expand its empire into the New World led to the conquest, enslavement, and eventual conversion of many Indians to Christianity. This illustration by 16th-century priest Diego Duran illustrates the warm reception the Spanish first received from the Aztec people in Mexico.

In the year 1492, Christopher Columbus, exploring for Spain, sighted the island of Española (now known as Hispaniola, which today is shared by the Dominican Republic and Haiti.) The Spanish conquered the Taino tribe that inhabited the island and established a European settlement there. Next, the Spanish took control of Puerto Rico, Jamaica, and Cuba from the natives. In 1521, they conquered the land which they called New Spain (present-day Mexico), destroying the Aztec civilization. The Spanish then headed to what is now the United States. One of these Spanish adventurers was Pánfilo de Narváez. His second in command was Álvar Núñez Cabeza de Vaca.

CABEZA DE VACA

The expedition led by Pánfilo de Narváez arrived on Española in early autumn of 1527. The crew

The SEVEN CITIES of GOLD

THE LEGEND OF THE SEVEN Cities of Gold began as a popular tale in medieval Spain. According to the story, seven bishops fled Spain just before the Moors, Muslims from northwest Africa, invaded in 711. Sailing west, they eventually reached a mythical island called Antilia. There, they each built a fabulous city, overflowing with gold, silver, and all manner of treasure. When Christopher Columbus landed in the West Indies in 1492, Europeans thought he had found Antilia, and so the West Indies came to be called the Antilles Islands.

spent the winter there and in Cuba. In April, five ships carrying 400 men sailed for Florida.

The decision by Narváez to split his men into two groups to explore Florida proved to be a huge mistake. The two parties were supposed to meet up again, but because Narváez's guides misjudged their geographic position, they never reunited. This left the group that included Narváez and Cabeza de Vaca with no support or supplies from the ships. Narváez also believed that his party was very close to Spanish territory in what is now northeastern Mexico where food and shelter would be found—but he was wrong. The men were actually lost in Florida more than 1,500 miles (2,414 km) from any help or supplies.

Cabeza de Vaca had argued against Narváez's plan, as he stated in his account of the journey, published in 1542:

> It seemed to me in no manner advisable to forsake the ships. I told him [Narváez] we had no interpreter to make ourselves understood by the natives. . . . Neither did we know what to expect from the land we were entering, having no knowledge of what it was . . . [and] finally, that we had not the supplies required for penetrating into an unknown country . . . so that, in my opinion, we should re-embark and sail in quest of a land and harbor better adapted to settlement.

But Narváez took his men inland and never saw his ships again. Many of the men died from Indian attacks, starvation, and disease.

The survivors, including Narváez and Cabeza de Vaca, made their way back to the coast and decided to try to escape by sea. The men built rafts from deerskins and tree branches. They killed the horses they had brought with them, and lived on their meat while constructing the rafts. Horsehide taken from the animals' legs was made into bags for carrying fresh water. Using their shirts for sails, the men took to the sea on five large rafts, hoping to reach a Spanish settlement called Pánuco, in New Spain.

HORSES *in* North America

WHEN THE SPANISH EXPLORERS AND conquistadores arrived in North and Central America in the late 15th and early 16th centuries, they brought horses with them. Horses had vanished from the continent 10,000 years earlier. Hernán Cortés and his army, who landed in Mexico in 1519, are generally credited with reintroducing horses to North America. The horses bred freely, and their numbers increased. The term "mustang" which comes from the Spanish word *mesteño*, means "ownerless beast." A mustang was a wild horse that roamed the continent in the years after the Spanish arrival.

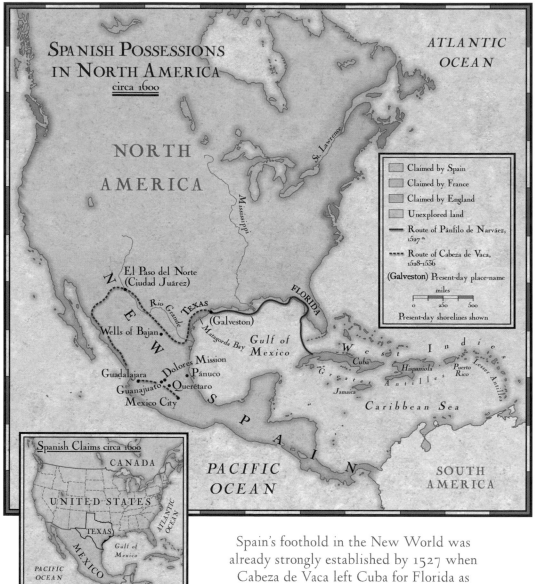

Spain's foothold in the New World was already strongly established by 1527 when Cabeza de Vaca left Cuba for Florida as part of an expedition that would eventually make him the first European to set foot in what is now Texas. The claims of England and France were concentrated far to the northeast and at the time were of little concern to Spain.

Two hundred fifty men set sail, but supplies soon ran thin. Cabeza de Vaca reported: *"Every day our thirst and hunger increased because our supplies were giving out. . . for the pouches we had made from the legs of our horses soon became rotten and useless."*

About a month into their journey, a huge storm struck, tearing the makeshift craft into driftwood. Narváez told his men that *"each must do as he thought best to save himself."* Cabeza de Vaca and 50 surviving comrades washed up on the shores of what is now Texas.

Most of the survivors were killed by disease, injuries, and violence at the hands of Indian tribes. Cabeza de Vaca survived, along with three companions. During their travels in Texas, Cabeza de Vaca and his comrades were captured and spent 18 months as slaves of the Mariame and Yguaze Indians before they managed to escape. Cabeza de Vaca was the first Spaniard to live among the Indians in Texas and to write extensively about his experiences.

When they finally reached Mexico City, the capital of New Spain, in 1536, Cabeza de Vaca and the others spoke of their eight-year journey through the area north of the known territory of New Spain.

Cabeza de Vaca told the viceroy of New Spain that the region that would become Texas had no great Indian nations, nor any precious metals or treasure. Based on a report he presented to the King of Spain, the Spanish decided not to colonize Texas—for now. ▨

viceroy—the governor of a colony or country, ruling in the name of a king or queen

CHAPTER TWO

Return to Texas

WHEN SPAIN'S RIVAL FRANCE establishes a colony near the Gulf of Mexico, the Spanish become interested in Texas again and send Alonso de León to find the French settlement.

rench explorer René-Robert Cavelier, Sieur de La Salle, peered out from the deck of his great sailing ship, *L'Aimable*. He was on his way to establish a French colony at the mouth of the Mississippi River on the Gulf of Mexico. The year was 1685, more than 150 years after Cabeza de Vaca had landed in Texas. The French king, Louis XIV, had asked La Salle to set up a colony in this key location in order to create a French presence for commerce in the area.

OPPOSITE: Sieur de La Salle's ship, *L'Aimable*, unloads supplies along the shores of Matagorda Bay in hopes of establishing a French presence in the region.

La Salle had charted the Gulf Coast three years before, but navigational errors caused him to sail past the mouth of the Mississippi. He continued sailing and found himself some 400 miles (640 km) west of the river he had hoped to find. When a storm struck, *L'Aimable* ran aground in the shallow waters of Matagorda Bay. Most of the cargo was lost. Crew member Henri Joutel wrote of the shipwreck in his journal: *"The ship was stranded on the shoals, and all the light goods were carry'd out by the water. This misfortune was so much the greater, because the vessel contain'd almost all of the ammunition, utensils, tools, and other necessaries for Monsr. de la Sale's enterprize and settlement."*

According to Joutel's journal, the settlers managed to salvage *"30 casks of wine and brandy, and some flesh [meat], and grain."* La Salle and about 180 crew members and colonists made it ashore with these minimal supplies. They began building a fort there on Matagorda Bay, founding the French colony of Fort St. Louis. As Joutel described it, *"We fell to work to make a fort, of the wreck of the ship that had been cast away and the pieces of timber the seas threw up."* During this difficult labor, many colonists died from overwork and starvation.

Joutel reported that almost as soon as La Salle's party landed, *"about an hundred and twenty of the natives came to our camp, with their bows and arrows."* La Salle offered to trade what little the French had, such as knives and other metal objects. In exchange, the Indians gave the colonists meat to eat and goatskins for clothing.

WHY DID THEY STARVE?

ACCORDING TO HENRI JOUTEL, THE LAND LA SALLE AND HIS fellow colonists found was abundant with wildlife.

We had an infinite number of wild goats, rabbits, turkeys, geese, swans, and partridges. The River supply'd us with an abundance of fishes. . . . The sea afforded us oysters and eels. We had plenty of land and sea tortoises, snakes, and toads. There were also many alligators in the rivers.

To this day, historians find it odd that the colonists complained of starvation when fish and fowl were apparently plentiful. Most historians believe that the colonists yearned for more familiar European food, such as wheat bread, olive oil, and beef. They felt that the "exotic" birds, fish, and lizards were fine for the local Indians, but not for them.

La Salle made several journeys to search for the Mississippi River. On one of these journeys, in 1687, his men staged a mutiny and murdered him. Some of the men had distrusted La Salle from the start of their voyage, questioning his ability to lead. This suspicion, coupled with their growing frustration regarding

mutiny—a refusal to obey a person in authority, with or without the use of force

yet another difficult and unsuccessful search for the Mississippi, led to the mutiny and murder. Without La Salle, the colony of Fort St. Louis faltered and was soon abandoned. The settlement quickly fell into ruins.

La Salle and a priest (who was part of his crew) confront the bodies of other members of his expedition sent out earlier to retrieve men who were hoarding food from the rest of the crew. Plotting to kill La Salle and stage a mutiny, an assassin hides in the bushes to the left in the painting, waiting for a moment to murder the French captain.

The Return
of the Spanish

The nations of France and Spain were rivals in Europe and in their quests to colonize the New World. Each saw itself as deserving to control the new frontier of America.

Already established in Mexico, the Caribbean, and Florida, Spain wanted to create colonies north of Mexico in the land that would one day be the United States. At this time, France had established profitable fur-trading settlements from Canada down to the mouth of the Mississippi River. The conflict between the two nations would lead to clashes over the land that would become Texas.

La Salle's last expedition had proved disastrous, but it planted the seeds for a Spanish return to Texas. Some of La Salle's crew had deserted before he reached Texas and found refuge in the Spanish colony of Santo Domingo on the island of Hispaniola. These crew members revealed La Salle's plans to establish a French colony at the mouth of the Mississippi. Word of his expedition reached Spanish officials in Europe in the summer of 1685.

The Spanish worried that a French presence on the Gulf of Mexico would pose a threat to Spanish commerce in Gulf waters, to Spanish settlements and mines in northern Mexico, and to the Spanish colony in Florida. They decided to try to find La Salle and stop him. This search was led by a frontiersman named Alonso de León.

Alonso de León

Schooled in Spain and trained by the Spanish Navy, Alonso de León led a series of explorations of the northern portions of New Spain from the 1660s until the mid-1680s. He was a seasoned outdoorsman and a skilled entrepreneur. Having gained great respect among Spanish leaders, de León used this influence to secure permission to work salt mines, open trade with settlements, and explore for silver mines in northern New Spain, increasing his personal wealth. When the time came for a Spanish return to Texas, de León was a logical choice to lead the way.

In March 1689, de León set out from New Spain with a party of 114 men on an expedition to Fort St. Louis. The soldiers, servants, mule drivers, and a priest named Damián Massanet trekked through the dry, barren countryside for a month.

Shortly before noon on April 22, 1689, de León found the ruins of Fort St. Louis. Father Massanet described it this way in his diary: "We . . . found six houses, not very large . . . and a wooden fort made from the hulk of a wrecked vessel. There was a great lot of shattered weapons, broken by the Indians. We found two unburied bodies, which I interred [buried]. . . . There were many torn up books and many dead pigs."

De León learned from the Tonkawa Indians that the Karankawa Indians, angry at the French colonists for stealing some of their canoes, had taken their revenge on the fort. What the Karankawa hadn't stolen from the settlement, they had destroyed.

The following day, de León and his soldiers found the remains of La Salle's ship, *L'Aimable*. On the return trip to his camp, de León encountered a group of Indians. To his shock, he discovered that two of them were actually Frenchmen, survivors of La Salle's settlement. Having fled the failed colony, the two Frenchmen had turned to the Indians to avoid starving to death. The Indians treated them cruelly, forcing them to do slave labor under the threat of punishment or death.

In his personal diary, Alonso de León described what the two Frenchmen told him.

Five Indians had come to the settlement. The Frenchmen, having no suspicions, went unarmed to see them. Once inside, other Indians kept coming and embracing them. Then another party of Indians came from the creek and killed them all, including a priest. . . . They [the two Frenchmen] were not there at the time, but they came back, finding their companions dead. They buried them, then exploded nearly a hundred barrels of powder so that the Indians could not carry it off.

CHAPTER THREE

First Settlements

With help from Alonso de León, Father Damián Massanet establishes the first Spanish mission in Texas and begins converting the Indians to Christianity.

 hen Alonso de León sent the account of his expedition back to Spain, Spanish officials realized that, at least for the moment, France did not pose a threat to their interests in the New World. Once they no longer had to protect their trading opportunities, the Spanish were free to focus on spreading Christianity to the Indians of New Spain, which now included the land that would become Texas. This task fell to Father Damián Massanet, with help from de León. Their expedition would lead to the establishment of the first permanent Spanish settlement in Texas.

OPPOSITE: Father Antonio Margil de Jesús was one of several Franciscan friars who preached to the region's natives, hoping to convert them to Christianity. He founded the mission San José near Villa de Béxar (San Antonio).

THE FIRST MISSION

In 1690, Alonso de León and Father Massanet led a small party of soldiers and priests in search of a suitable spot for a mission. A mission was a settlement in which priests called missionaries worked to convert natives to Christianity. The natives lived with the priests at the mission, studied the Bible, and helped with everyday tasks such as farming, hunting, and cooking.

It was once believed that missions were harmonious communities in which Indians worked side by side with humane priests, while studying the Bible. More recently, historians have come to believe that many Indians in the Spanish missions were exploited as slave laborers, forced to construct buildings and create goods, such as woven blankets, for the missions to sell.

After crossing the Rio Grande and eventually reaching the Neches River, the expedition encountered a settlement of Caddo Indians. Previous missionaries who had not established permanent colonies had paved the way for the natives' acceptance of Christianity, and they welcomed a permanent mission. Alonso de León described the Caddo in his account of the journey: *"The Indians lived in houses furnished with wooden benches and raised canopied beds, and they possessed a large quantity of pots and earthen jars for cooking, as well as stones for grinding corn into meal."*

Father Massanet was immediately impressed by the location. He wrote in his diary, *"We found a delightful spot close to the brook, fine woods, with plum trees like those in Spain. On that very day we began to fell trees and cart the wood, and within three days we had a roomy dwelling and a church."* San Francisco de los Tejas was the first permanent Spanish settlement in Texas. It was established, among the Caddo Indians, on the site of present-day Augusta, Texas. The Spanish and Indians soon were sharing meals together.

PERMANENT SETTLEMENT BEGINS

Father Francisco Hidalgo worked with Father Massanet at the San Francisco de los Tejas settlement. In 1700, Hidalgo established the mission San Juan Bautista near the Rio Grande. For the next decade, Hidalgo tried to convince Spanish officials to allow him to create additional missions, but the Spanish had once again lost interest in Texas, because it remained difficult and expensive to settle. Father Hidalgo turned to the French.

Tejas
TEXAS

THE WORD "TEJAS," THE CADDO word for "friend" or "ally," is the name by which the Caddo addressed each other. Over time, the Spanish began using the word "Tejas" to describe the area. Later, when the Americans arrived, the word was anglicized to "Texas," the name of the colony, the republic, and the state.

Father Francisco Hidalgo

Francisco Hidalgo, the most determined and dedicated Spanish missionary in early Texas, was born in Spain in 1659. In 1683, Hidalgo was part of a group of 23 priests who sailed from Spain to found the College of Santa Cruz de Querétaro in New Spain, near the current town of Querétaro in Mexico. The college was the first institution in North America established for the teaching of the Catholic faith. By 1688, Hidalgo had left the college to begin active missionary work among the Indians. After establishing missions in East Texas, he moved to the San Antonio de Valero Mission in San Antonio in 1719. He died in 1726.

In 1711, Hidalgo wrote a letter to the French governor of Louisiana describing his frustration in trying to convince the Spanish authorities to establish additional missions. *"Seeing that all the means I had taken had failed, a happy thought occurred to me,"* he wrote. That "happy thought" was to invite the French to establish a mission in East Texas in the region close to French Louisiana. Hidalgo was hoping that this action by the French would once again cause the Spanish government to react by establishing more missions of its own.

The governor of Louisiana, Antoine de La Mothe, Sieur de Cadillac, was only too happy to oblige, seeing an opportunity for French expansion. He also hoped to tempt Spanish settlers to buy French goods in nearby Louisiana, since the Spanish did not allow French goods into New Spain.

sieur—an archaic French title, comparable to "sir"

The governor sent an experienced soldier and explorer named Louis Juchereau de Saint-Denis to establish a mission in Natchitoches, near Louisiana's border with Texas. The mission was founded in 1714, followed shortly by the establishment of Fort St. Jean Baptiste to protect the settlement.

The French response to Father Hidalgo had the desired effect. Spanish commandant Diego Ramón told Hidalgo, *"if His Majesty does not intervene, the French will be masters of all this land."* Spanish leaders in Mexico City agreed. They ordered the establishment of a settlement in East Texas to act as a buffer against the French.

In April 1716, about 75 people led by Ramón set out from Mexico City on an expedition to establish a Spanish colony in East Texas. Among this group was Father Hidalgo himself, along with nine other Franciscan priests, 26 soldiers, and several dozen civilian colonists, including three children six years old or younger and seven women.

presidio—a Spanish fort or military post

The group found a location near the Louisiana border where they built four small wooden churches and the presidio of

San Francisco de los Dolores. Although the mission and the presidio would eventually fall under the pressure of Indian attacks, they represented another step in the permanent Spanish settlement of Texas.

SAN ANTONIO

In 1716, shortly after Ramón's expedition, the viceroy of New Spain, Baltasar de Zúñiga y Guzmán, the Marqués de Valero, named a former sailor in the Royal Spanish Navy, Martín de Alarcón, as governor of Texas. The viceroy wanted to establish a settlement along the San Antonio River, near Matagorda Bay, not far from where La Salle had landed. Valero sent Alarcón and Father Antonio de San Buenaventura y Olivares to found a mission and presidio near the headwaters of the San Antonio River.

Father Olivares had been thinking of settling this location for more than a decade. After an earlier trip into Texas, Olivares had never forgotten the place, noting in a diary that San Pedro Creek, which flowed into the San Antonio River, *could supply not only a village but a city.* In the spring of 1718, Olivares and Alarcón set out from Mexico City with soldiers, priests, an engineer, a stone mason, a blacksmith, and a group of women and children.

Arriving in early May, the group founded a mission, San Antonio de Valero (the mission's chapel would one day be known as the Alamo), and a presidio, San Antonio de

Béxar. Together, the mission and the presidio formed the Villa de Béxar. It would become the most important town in Spanish Texas, known today as San Antonio.

The mission San Antonio de Valero, which became known as the Alamo, was a center of activity for the settlers who lived in Villa de Béxar, known today as San Antonio.

Father Francisco Celiz, another priest at the mission kept a record of Villa de Béxar's early days. He wrote,

> The settlers' early attempts to locate sites on the river where water could be diverted for crops proved unsuccessful. However by the following January, at least one appropriate site on the river and one on the creek had been found, and work on the acequias [irrigation ditches] for the town and mission began. The settlers completed the work successfully and now expect a large crop of maize [corn], beans, and vegetables.

Leaving the colonists at San Antonio to do their planting, Alarcón set out with a group of soldiers to check on Father Hidalgo's missions in East Texas. Arriving at San Francisco de los Dolores, Alarcón was shocked to discover that the missions, only a few years old, were on the verge of collapse.

Alarcón learned that supplies had run low, and attacks by the Hasinais Indians, armed by the French, had increased. The soldiers at the presidio of San Francisco de los Dolores, which had been set up to protect the missions, had deserted. The priests who remained were starving. Alarcón brought fresh supplies and offered gifts to the Hasinais, but, eventually, the eastern missions were abandoned.

Life back at Villa de Béxar remained peaceful until the Apache Indians attacked in 1720. For generations, the Apache had lived the lives of farmers and hunters. They planted crops in the spring and hunted buffalo in the fall and winter. By mid-1720, raiding Comanche warriors had taken over the hunting grounds and farm lands of the Apache tribe. Unable to grow food or hunt, the Apache turned to raiding settlements.

The Spanish sent more soldiers. Soon, the presidio had more than 50 troops, who managed to defeat the natives. Spanish officials sent Inspector General Pedro de Rivera y Villalón to check on the effectiveness of the military force. He reported, "*This presidio is garrisoned by a captain and fifty-three soldiers, but a smaller number would easily suffice. The only enemies in the area are a few Apaches, who know from experience how efficiently the soldiers perform their duty.*"

Governor Alarcón had succeeded in founding a colony based on the instructions given to him by the viceroy of New Spain. The viceroy had said: "*It must be recognized that these settlements must be the rampart, fortress and defense of all this New Spain.*" No town would be the scene of more important battles in the history of Texas than Villa de Béxar. ✳

OPPOSITE: Little Spaniard was a member of the Comanche tribe, Native Americans who threatened Spanish settlers and neighboring Indian tribes alike.

The Growth of Permanent Settlements

MARQUÉS DE SAN MIGUEL AGUAYO *brings soldiers and livestock into Texas. He reestablishes six missions, constructs two more, and builds two new presidios.*

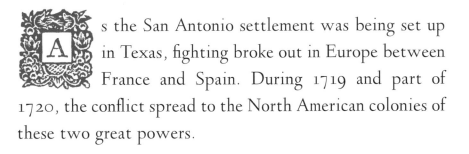 s the San Antonio settlement was being set up in Texas, fighting broke out in Europe between France and Spain. During 1719 and part of 1720, the conflict spread to the North American colonies of these two great powers.

OPPOSITE: This mission, founded in 1720, was named in Honor of Saint Joseph (San José) and the Marqués de San Miguel de Aguayo. Aguayo is credited with firmly establishing Texas as a Spanish colony and encouraging the growth of settlements there.

In June 1719, a force of French soldiers from Natchitoches, along with pro-French Caddo Indians, stormed the six missions and presidio in East Texas. The Spanish colonists, missionaries, and soldiers fled to San Antonio.

King Felipe V of Spain was furious. He wanted to secure Spain's claim on Texas once and for all. A wealthy Spanish nobleman, José de Azlor y Virto de Vera, the Marqués de San Miguel de Aguayo, had been petitioning the viceroy of New Spain to allow him to lead an expedition into Texas. When the viceroy received word from the king of Spain that Texas was to be secured, he gave permission to Aguayo to depart.

Aguayo was to reestablish Spanish control of the missions and reinforce the presidio in East Texas to keep the French out permanently, then head west to create a Spanish presence across Texas. In the fall of 1719, Aguayo was named the new governor of Texas, replacing Martín de Alarcón. Plans began for a massive invasion of the territory. Aguayo's march would result in the permanent Spanish colonization of all of Texas.

In the spring of 1721, the ground shook as an army of 500 soldiers, 2,800 horses, 4,800 cattle, and 6,400 sheep and goats stormed into Texas. Aguayo's massive march was the first cattle drive in the history of the state. The arrival of these huge herds of livestock marked the beginning of ranching in Texas.

Cattle drives are believed to have originated with the
Marqués de San Miguel de Aguayo, who arrived in Texas with
almost 5,000 head of cattle trailing his army.

This group of men and animals confronted Louis
Juchereau de Saint-Denis at Texas' border with Louisiana,
near French Natchitoches. Under orders from the French
government, Saint-Denis was planning a raid on San
Antonio. Confronted by Aguayo's superior force, however,
Saint-Denis retreated to Louisiana.

Aguayo's expedition immediately went to work
reopening the six East Texas missions and presidio that had
been abandoned two years earlier. In addition, Aguayo
built another presidio, Nuestra Señora del Pilar de Los
Adaes, just 12 miles (19 km) from Natchitoches. Before
moving on to the west, Aguayo left 100 soldiers and 6
cannon behind at the new fortress. Los Adaes became the
first capital of Spanish Texas.

Aguayo's army marched southwest toward San Antonio, pausing at Matagorda Bay. Sifting through the rubble of the ruined Fort St. Louis, one of Aguayo's party reported that *"we found nails, pieces of gun locks, and fragments of other items used by the French."* There, on that very site, Aguayo began construction of another presidio, because he considered this to be another location vulnerable to French attack. Leaving a crew to complete the new fort, called Nuestra Señora de la Bahía del Espíritu Santo (also known as "La Bahía"), he continued on to San Antonio.

By the time Aguayo left Texas in 1722, he had reestablished six missions, constructed two more, built two new presidios, and increased the number of Spanish soldiers from 50 to 268. He returned to the viceroy in Mexico City with a proposal that new civilian settlements be established in the area between East Texas and San Antonio. He suggested that 400 families be brought in from Spanish possessions like the Canary Islands (off the northwest coast of Africa) and Havana, Cuba.

CANARY ISLAND SETTLERS

King Felipe took Aguayo's advice and encouraged civilians to settle in Texas. The king believed that more civilians would mean less need for expensive presidios to protect the colonies. He figured that once the civilians were there, they would defend themselves and their land out of self-preservation.

Colonists from the Canary Islands had successfully emigrated to other parts of New Spain to escape difficult economic times. Now, in March 1731, 14 families made up of 55 people arrived in San Antonio to begin a new life in Texas. The king of Spain had paid for their journey. A total of 400 Canary Islanders were supposed to come, but the colonization of the first group proved more costly than the Spanish government expected, and no others were sent.

The new arrivals founded the town of San Fernando de Béxar, near the existing presidio at San Antonio. Most of the new colonists had been laborers, farmers, and fishermen. Right from the start, these newcomers, known as Isleños, began quarreling with their neighbors—the missionaries, soldiers, civilian settlers, and Indians who were already living in San Antonio. The Isleños refused to allow anyone else to live in their new town. They filed complaints and lawsuits against outsiders and even against each other. One official in Mexico City wrote of them,

> *The fourteen families from the Canary Islands complain against the reverend fathers of the five missions, against the Indians that reside therein . . . and against the other forty-nine families settled there, so that it seems that they desire to be left alone in undisputed possession. Perhaps even then they may not find enough room in the vast area of the entire province.*

The earlier settlers viewed the Isleños as inexperienced newcomers, unsuited to life on the frontier. The Isleños had no experience raising livestock or dealing with horses. Also, the Isleños' newly planted crops proved extremely tempting to the ranchers' grazing cattle, sheep, and goats. Unwilling to fence their fields to keep the animals out, the Isleños defended their crops by killing or injuring the live-stock. This upset the ranchers, many of whom were San Antonio's missionaries. Both sides argued and complained to the governor of Texas and the viceroy in Mexico City.

Another major cause of the conflicts was the fact that the Canary Islanders had been born in Spain, though they had later moved to the Canary Islands. Throughout the whole colonial period, Spanish-born Spaniards occupied the top posts in government and considered themselves socially superior to the Creoles. The Canary Islanders considered themselves superior to the soldiers and settlers already established in San Antonio. The Isleños arrived in San Antonio with privileges granted by the king of Spain, the most important of which was full control of the town's cabildo.

Creole—a person of European descent born in the West Indies or Spanish America

cabildo—a government advisory council in the Spanish colonies

Over the next few decades, Indian attacks forced the colonists to unite against a common enemy. Intermarriage also brought a blending of cultures to the colony, which grew and flourished. By the end of the century, San Antonio had more than 1,400 residents.

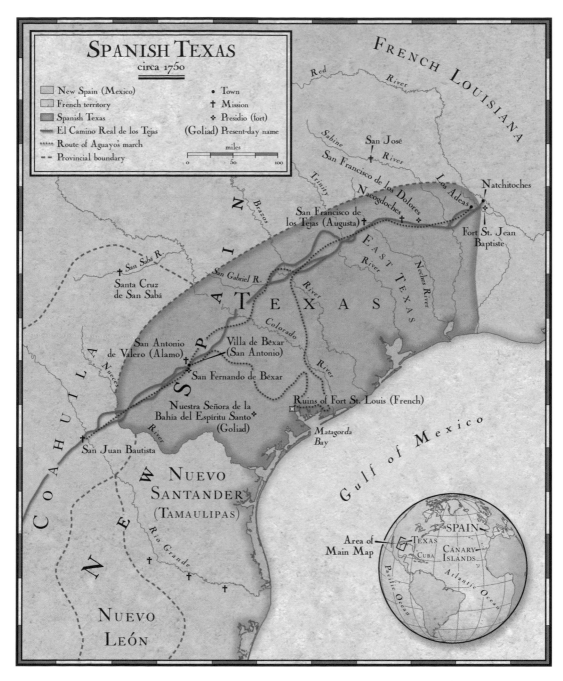

The 1719 march of the Marqués de San Miguel de Aguayo into Texas (dotted line) reestablished Spanish control of the region and to the colonization of all of Texas. El Camino Real (solid blue line) was the most important roadway of the time. The inset map shows how far the Canary Islanders traveled to settle in Texas.

El Camino Real

THE SPANISH COLONIES IN TEXAS STRETCHED from San Antonio in the west to the settlement of Nacogdoches (established in 1716) in the east. El Camino Real, "the king's highway" connected the settlements. Supplies, soldiers, and military equipment were transported along the route. It was used by ranchers for cattle drives, as well. Alonso de León's 1690 expedition to establish a mission in East Texas was the first to use it. Domingo Terán de los Ríos, the first governor of Spanish Texas, followed a year later, leading missionaries to the East Texas missions. Gregorio de Salinas Varona used the trail in 1693 to bring supplies to the missions. Eventually, immigrants from the United States made their way into Texas along El Camino Real, changing the region forever.

EXPANSION

Hoping to expand their work of spreading Christianity to the Indians, several priests sought to create new Spanish missions in Texas during the 1740s and 1750s. Most of these missions failed. Like those in East Texas, they suffered from a lack of financial support from Spain.

The task of converting the Indians proved much more difficult than it first appeared. For example, the mission Santa Cruz de San Sabá lasted less than a year. Despite a

A VIOLENT END

IN MARCH 1758, MEMBERS OF the Comanche staged an early morning raid on the mission at San Sabá. The priests woke up to find themselves surrounded by Indians armed with muskets, swords, and lances. Father Miguel Molina wrote of the experience, *"I saw nothing but Indians on every hand.... Besides the paint on their faces, red and black, they were adorned with the pelts and tails of wild beasts ... as well as deer horns."* The raiding Indians stole horses, killed eight priests, and set fire to the mission. Father Molina and twelve others escaped to the safety of the presidio.

flow of thousands of Apache right past the mission as they headed north to hunt buffalo, not a single one would ever enter the mission or be converted at San Sabá. Forced from their lands by the Comanche, the Apache became nomadic, moving from place to place in search of better hunting. This made them less open to conversion than the Caddo, whose farmland had not been threatened and who stayed in one place long enough for the missionaries to convert them. Some priests became disheartened and returned to San Antonio.

The growth of Spanish settlements in Texas was slow. Conflicts among settlers and the dangers of Indian attacks made development a grueling process fraught with many setbacks. For those living there, however, daily life went on amid the quarrels and perils. ✳

CHAPTER FIVE

Life in Spanish Texas

LIFE IN SPANISH TEXAS *includes priests and Indians in the missions, soldiers in the presidios, and families in the civilian settlements.*

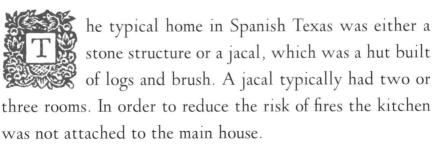

T he typical home in Spanish Texas was either a stone structure or a jacal, which was a hut built of logs and brush. A jacal typically had two or three rooms. In order to reduce the risk of fires the kitchen was not attached to the main house.

No home was complete without its vegetable garden, but the threat of Indian raids cast a shadow over even this basic part of colonial life. Though not as devastating as the frequent murder of ranchers, Indian garden raids frustrated settlers and depleted the settlements' food supplies. The

OPPOSITE: Texas farmers greet a neighbor on horseback outside their jacal, or hut, built of logs and brush cleared from the surrounding land.

governor of Texas noted that *"Indians had been in most of the gardens facing west where they destroyed untold watermelons, melons, squash and maize."*

Indian raids remained a problem throughout the 18th century. The Indians of Texas were neither conquered nor were all converted to Catholicism. The fiercely proud Comanche and Apache never submitted to the Spanish system of forced labor that came with conversion.

The governor of Spanish Texas during the 1740s, Tomás Winthuysen, visited the struggling missions of East Texas. He declared the conversion of the Tejas Indians of the area an impossible undertaking.

Some Indians genuinely adopted Catholicism as their faith. Some wanted no part of mission life. Others went along with the wishes of the missionaries, choosing to take their chances for survival under the protection of the Spanish soldiers living in the presidios, rather than facing warring tribes of the Apache and Comanche on their own.

THE MISSIONS

The system of setting up missions was developed as Spain expanded north from Mexico City during the 16th and 17th centuries. The missionaries' goal was to bring together a large number of Indians in one community. There, the missionaries taught a whole group of natives Catholicism and loyalty to Spain, as well as ranching and farming techniques that would help support the mission.

The missions consisted of a number of buildings used for church services, shops, and residences. The goal was for missions to be self-sufficient through farming and ranching, but that aim was hard to achieve. Missionaries in Texas complained regularly to the viceroy of New Spain that labor problems caused food shortages. They said that often there were not enough people to harvest crops or hunt wild game.

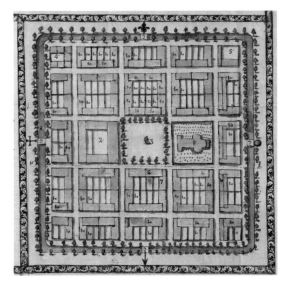

Spanish missions were centered on an *iglesia* [church] (#4 in the diagram above), which faced the plaza (#3) around which important government buildings were placed. This plan of San Antonio, Texas, is from a 1780 manuscript called *Memorias para la historia de la provincial Texas.*

One reason for this was widespread disease among the Indian converts. Like Indians in all the North American colonies, the natives of Texas had no immunity against European diseases. This cut down on the number of Indians able to work on the farms producing food.

The priests at the missions complained that others would fake illness in order to get out of work. They would, however, show up at mealtime, thus consuming food without helping to grow any. One missionary, not knowing who was really sick, wrote that he could "*neither force a sick man to work, nor be sure that those who use that pretext are really ill."* To escape the constant labor of mission life, some Indians left the settlements to join nearby tribes. The food shortages also affected the soldiers living in presidios and civilians living in settlements in the region, since the crops grown at the missions helped feed all of these people.

In this painting of 17th-century San Antonio by José Cisneros a priest looks over architectural drawings of the mission Conseption.

THE PRESIDIOS

Spanish presidios were originally built to provide safe passage for travelers between central Mexico and the silver-producing regions north of Mexico City. The presidios of Texas were the last in a long line of defensive posts that ran from Mexico City through the regions to the north and then into the dangerous frontier of northern Mexico, including Texas.

The presidios of Texas also protected the missions and Indians from attacks by enemy tribes. The commanders and common soldiers at the forts hoped to subdue hostile Indians by force, while the missionaries believed in subduing them by introducing them to the ideas of the church. Soldiers would sometimes mistreat mission Indians which upset the priests.

Both officers and common soldiers faced hardships in Texas. Most of the men who served as officers had come from upper-class society in Spain. Back home, they enjoyed privileges such as fine food, material goods such as clothing, jewelry, and furniture, and political power. In Texas, they found themselves on the primitive frontier, balancing the dangers of Indian attacks with the boredom of living in a remote place. Their leaders back in Mexico City and Madrid often criticized them for not doing a better job of protecting colonists from Indian attacks, and outright neglected them when funds ran low. Many officers turned to drinking and treated the soldiers under their command harshly.

Army life was even worse for the common soldier. He was on the front lines during Indian attacks and had little experience fighting natives. His duties were monotonous, his wages were pitiful, and abuse from his commanders was frequent. The average presidio soldier in Texas by the end of the 1700s was supposed to be earning a small salary plus a monthly supply of corn, sugar, beef, and pork. The soldier was expected to support himself and his family on this and pay for his equipment.

In reality, common soldiers rarely saw all of their salary. Those in charge of distributing the pay often spent the money themselves, leaving the troops deep in debt. A common soldier and his family lived on the verge of starvation. His military equipment also deteriorated, leaving him poorly equipped to do his job. Morale among the soldiers plummeted with each incident of stolen pay or broken rifle.

Soldiers were also charged with carrying out the sentences of those convicted of a crime. In the criminal justice system of Spanish Texas, any number of offenses were punished with the death penalty. These included treason, murder, witchcraft, dueling, and speaking out against the king, any member of the royal family, or the government of Spain.

treason—the crime of betraying one's country

Beatings and whippings, loss of half of one's property, or eight to ten years of imprisonment were the punishments for burglary, disrespecting a priest, concealing deserters, and using improper language. Anyone who encouraged a soldier to desert received 200 lashes and was forced to serve for six years without pay in the presidio where that soldier was stationed.

D A I L Y   L O G

THIS DAILY LOG FROM THE BÉXAR PRESIDIO AT SAN ANTONIO gives some idea of the mindless, boring routine faced by frontier soldiers. San Antonio was the "hot spot" of Spanish Texas. While dealing with boredom, these soldiers also faced the fear that a surprise Indian attack could strike at any moment.

BÉXAR PRESIDIAL REPORT—OCTOBER 1778

OCTOBER 3: The corporal and two soldiers returned with the mail pouch from the Presidio of Rio Grande.

OCTOBER 4: Three soldiers left to conduct a sealed envelope containing documents to the Presidio of Rio Grande.

OCTOBER 5: The sergeant and twelve men brought back the body of a dead native and buried it, not having learned to what tribe he belonged.

OCTOBER 7: A citizen arrived with the news that four Tonkawa chieftains had requested chewing tobacco.

OCTOBER 8: A corporal, a soldier who interprets, and four others left to deliver the tobacco to the Indians in the usual manner....

CIVILIAN SETTLEMENTS

Civilian settlers also lived on the frontier of Spanish Texas. These settlers forged a life for themselves by farming and ranching on the rugged frontier. As the colony grew, the number of children increased. Settlers became concerned about the lack of schools.

In 1789, a San Antonio resident, José Francisco de la Mata, offered to educate the children of the town teaching them reading, writing, obedience to their parents, loyalty to Spain, and commitment to Catholicism. He was granted the right to run a school. Soon the idea of schools in Texas spread. Commandant General Nemesio Salcedo of San Antonio wrote to the governor of Spanish Texas to request schools for all of Texas: *"I wish to procure such institutions in all presidios and posts where the number of inhabitants are sufficient."*

Despite these efforts on the part of a few individuals, a true public school system in Spanish Texas never developed. Most settlers in Spanish Texas, both adults and children, could not read or write. Those with means sent their children to school in Mexico or even Spain. Most other colonists had to be satisfied with the teachings of the priests to educate their children. Most of these children worked hard on farms and ranches and were not immune to the harshness and dangers of life in Spanish Texas, such as Indian attacks, brutal heat, and poverty.

Colonial life in Texas was not all work, however. Most celebrations centered on organized religious feasts. In San Antonio, December, with its feasts of the Immaculate Conception and Our Lady of Guadalupe, was the most socially active month. The residents enjoyed big meals, bullfights, games, and dances. These festivals were held during the month in between the late maize harvest and the cattle branding and preparations for new plantings. The festivals offered an opportunity to celebrate another year of existence as a community.

ECONOMY AND INDUSTRY

Farming and ranching were the mainstays of the economy of Spanish Texas. Although mission-aries operated a silver mine near El Paso del Norte from the late

As more and more settlers turned to ranching, cowboys became known for their horsemanship. In this painting, a cowboy cuts, or separates, a calf from the herd.

1700s until Mexican independence in 1821, mining was not a major economic factor in Spanish Texas. As the colony grew, artisans arrived, including tailors, carpenters, black-smiths, gunsmiths, and construction workers. Many of these people also farmed or worked on ranches to supple-ment their income or provide food for themselves.

Texas was slow in creating transportation and manufac-turing industries because of the great distances between set-tlements and the difficulty and expense of developing the region. Some of the rivers provided a means of transporting goods, but even the largest rivers were unreliable due to periodic low water, sandbars, and blockages.

Lumber mills and flour mills operated on the local level. Bricks and items for horses, such as harnesses and saddles, were also made. The size of Texas and the difficulties in transporting goods limited these businesses to small areas.

SPAIN GETS LOUISIANA

The French and Indian War (1754–1763) was a struggle between France and Great Britain to see who would be the dominant colonial power in eastern North America. Near the end of the war, King Carlos III of Spain worried that a victorious Britain would next turn its eyes toward Spain's colonies. Therefore, Spain formed an alliance with its longtime enemy, France. Even the combined might of France and Spain was not enough to stop the British, however.

Spain did not want to see the British control French Louisiana, which bordered Texas. Carlos III now saw Britain as a much greater threat to Spanish interests than France had been. France, meanwhile, had considered Louisiana more trouble than it was worth for years. At the peace conference after the French and Indian War, a deal was struck among the three great powers in 1763. Spain took possession of the part of Louisiana that was west of the Mississippi River, including its main port, New Orleans.

"NEW REGULATIONS FOR PRESIDIOS"

The 1763 Treaty of Paris removed France from mainland North America (the French still had islands in the Caribbean and two islands off Canada) and left Britain as the only challenger to Spain's power on the continent. King Carlos III quickly turned his attention to the defense of New Spain and its borders. He sent Cayetano María Pignatelli Rubí Corbera y Saint Climent, the Marqués de Rubí, to conduct inspection tours of the frontier. Rubí traveled thousands of miles, visiting presidios and checking on their readiness to defend New Spain.

Rubí's report, delivered to the king in 1767, was bleak. He told the king that *"with rare exceptions, the northern frontier presidios were military mockeries: crumbling structures, incompetently and corruptly managed."* Rubí recommended major changes in the setup of the presidios in Texas. He also questioned the value of the missions. Many had not converted a single Indian in years, yet they were very expensive to defend.

In 1772, Carlos III finally put Rubí's recommendations into effect. On September 10, he issued a royal order called the "New Regulations for Presidios." This ordered the abandonment of all presidios in Texas except for those at San Antonio and La Bahía (later known as Goliad). In addition, the edict required everyone in East Texas to move to San Antonio, which was made the capital of Texas.

Presidios, missions, and civilian homes, ranches, and farms were to be abandoned. Moving all Spanish settlers from East Texas to San Antonio was no easy task. The population of settlers in the area had grown from 200 in 1767 to 500 at the time of the orders to move.

Governor Juan María de Ripperdá arrived in the summer of 1773 and told the settlers to prepare to move to San Antonio in a week. When they reached San Antonio, they found themselves in an unfamiliar place competing for good farmland.

The settlers petitioned Governor Ripperdá to allow them to return to East Texas. Ripperdá contacted the viceroy of New Spain, Antonio María de Bucareli y Ursúa, who agreed to allow the settlers to establish a new home back east. Although some stayed in San Antonio, many headed back. They chose a spot along El Camino Real near the Trinity River, about 300 miles (480 km) west of the abandoned mission at Nacogdoches. They named the settlement Bucareli in honor of the viceroy.

Unfortunately, this new settlement lasted only four years. A combination of flooding and repeated Comanche attacks forced the settlers to abandon their new home. Without any permission from the government, the colonists moved to the former mission at Nacogdoches. From that point in 1779, Nacogdoches remained a permanent Texas settlement, and in 1795, the Spanish government sent troops to defend the town.

BOOM TIME IN SAN ANTONIO

Meanwhile soldiers and settlers poured into San Antonio during 1773. Its economic life improved and the ability of the presidio to provide defense grew stronger. As the city prospered, it became more attractive to new settlers. The population of San Antonio nearly doubled between 1770 and 1780.

The Military Plaza of the presidio at the Mission San Antonio de Béxar

In addition to the relocated settlers from East Texas, settlers came from the interior of New Spain, as well as from Canada, France, Ireland, and, of course, Spain itself. Peace treaties signed with the Comanche in 1785 encouraged the return of ranchers and made the prospect of living in San

Antonio even more appealing. As the missions faded due to the lack of success in converting many Indians to Christianity, more civilians arrived. They replaced converted Indians as the primary labor force.

The First
CENSUS
REPORTS

CENSUS REPORTS FROM 1777 TO 1793 LISTED THE LARGEST part of the population in Texas settlements—approximately 50 percent—simply as "Spaniards." No distinction was made between Spanish-born Spaniards and American-born Spaniards. Indians, listed at 29.5 percent, made up the second-largest segment of the population in 1777. In 1793, that number was down to 8.6 percent. By that time, missionary activity among the Indians was on the decline, and more civilian colonists (farmers and ranchers) than converted Indians lived in the settlements.

In 1777, blacks made up less than 1 percent of the population, totaling just 20 people. By 1793 there were still fewer than 40. Most of these were probably slaves. Spanish settlers in Texas had very few slaves because the governments of Spain and, later, Mexico were firmly against the institution.

The 1792 census listed a total of 2,992 people living in Texas—1,617 males and 1,375 females. The only additional breakdown it gives is that there were 247 male mulattoes, 167 female mulattoes, 15 black males, and 19 black females.

A census report in 1782 broke down the population of San Antonio into official categories: Spaniards (born in Spain), blacks (mostly slaves), Indians, mestizos, and mulattos. Unofficially, the social order in Spanish Texas broke down into even more subgroups.

mestizo—a person born of Spanish and Native American parents in early Spanish colonies; often, a derogatory term

mulatto—a person born of Spanish and black parents in early Spanish colonies; often, a derogatory term

peninsular—a Spaniard in the early Spanish colonies who had been born in Spain

At the top of the social pyramid were the peninsulares. Next on the social ladder were the Creoles, followed by the mestizos, mulattos, Indians who had been converted and had adopted the customs of the Spanish, and, finally, blacks. These distinctions largely determined who ran the government, held positions of authority, and benefited most from any money that came into the colony. These social classes would also play a large role when the rumblings of revolution began early in the next century.

Because settlements in Spanish Texas were so isolated, intermarriage among the various groups in each was far more common than in the former British colonies of the newly independent United States. (The British colonies had won their independence in 1783, becoming the United States of America.) Within a few decades, this change would be one of the factors that caused New Spain to explode into revolution. ※

CHAPTER SIX

Mexican Independence

AFTER 300 YEARS OF SPANISH CONTROL, *Mexico, revolts against the tyranny of Spanish kings and becomes an independent nation.*

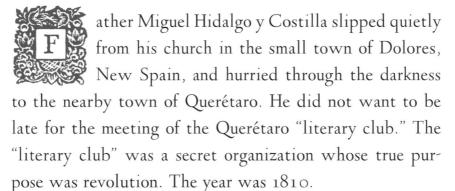

Father Miguel Hidalgo y Costilla slipped quietly from his church in the small town of Dolores, New Spain, and hurried through the darkness to the nearby town of Querétaro. He did not want to be late for the meeting of the Querétaro "literary club." The "literary club" was a secret organization whose true purpose was revolution. The year was 1810.

For years, Father Hidalgo had called the kings of Spain tyrants. He was a strong supporter of the rights of Creoles, mestizos, and Indians, who he felt were oppressed under

OPPOSITE: This painting of Father Miguel Hidalgo y Costilla, a priest and revolutionary, was done by artist A. Vargas in 1900.

the rule of the peninsulares. The peninsulares held all of the top political offices in the Spanish colonies and received favors from the Spanish king and the viceroy of New Spain. They viewed themselves as superior to other social classes.

Spain had looked to its colonies for help when it ran up war debts during continuing conflicts with France in Europe. The Spanish government seized assets of the church and colonies for its own use. Hidalgo likened this action to the unfair taxation of the American colonists by the British after the French and Indian War. In the preamble to Hidalgo's 1810 proclamation for self-government, he wrote of the Americans' struggle: "*From the moment in which the courageous American Nation took arms in order to throw off the heavy yoke that pressed down on her . . . one of the principal objects was to extinguish the many taxes which prevented her fortune from progressing.*" He also called for the end of slavery.

Hidalgo appealed to Creole soldiers to join his militia: "*To arms, Americans [referring to the Creoles, who had been born in America, not Spain]. . . . The enemy is weak and without resources. Recognize your duty, join the party of your Nation, reject that servile and shameful fear which makes you fight under the very banners that you abhor.*"

militia—a group of citizen-soldiers

Although some racial intermarriage into the upper classes did take place in New Spain, most mestizos, mulattoes, Indians, and blacks were still poor laborers or slaves, working long hours for little or no pay in the fields, mines, and houses of the privileged peninsulares. These groups, hoping to improve their lives, supported the Creoles in their desire for independence and control of their own country. Most believed that if Creoles were in positions of power, then life would improve for the lower classes.

At the regular meetings of the Querétaro "literary club," Hidalgo and his fellow rebels were plotting the separation of New Spain from the rule of its European parent. The battles that would follow would be the first steps toward an independent Mexico, free from Spanish rule.

By the spring of 1810, a plan was in place for an uprising to be held that December. However, by summer, details of this plan, called the "Querétaro Conspiracy," was known by too many people, including the viceroy in Mexico City. In September, he sent soldiers to Dolores to arrest the conspirators. The revolution ended before it had even begun.

A rebel named Juan de Aldama got word of the impending arrests. Riding with all speed through the night, Aldama—who became known as the Paul Revere of Mexican independence for his nighttime gallop— arrived in Dolores in the early morning hours of September 16.

An engraving of revolutionary Juan de Aldama

He told Hidalgo and the other conspirators about the soldiers who were on their way.

The rebels had no choice but to start their revolution that night, two months early. They quickly recruited thousands of untrained Indians and mestizos to join in their cause. Because Hidalgo was popular among these groups and spoke their languages, he was the natural choice to lead the rebellion. Unfortunately, the man who would be known as the father of Mexican independence was not very good at organizing and planning.

The ragtag rebels swept into the town of Guanajuato. Their sheer numbers quickly overwhelmed a force of royalists. Then the Indians and mestizos, along with Creoles, releasing years of pent-up hatred for the peninsulares, destroyed the town and murdered everyone in their path.

royalist—a colonist who remained loyal to the crown of Spain

The rebels moved on to Mexico City. After defeating royalists just outside the city, Hidalgo, for unknown reasons, chose not to invade Mexico City itself. This decision caused great tension within the ranks of his followers.

The last major battle of Hidalgo's revolt took place 30 miles (48 km) east of Guadalajara on January 17, 1811. What appeared to be a victory for the rebels turned suddenly into a crushing defeat when a grass fire blazed out of control. Panic swept through the rebel ranks along with the flames, and Hidalgo's soldiers scattered. Hidalgo himself fled north.

In the summer of 1811, royalist soldiers finally caught Hidalgo at Wells of Bajan in the province of Coahuila, just south of Texas. He was executed, but the spark of revolution would spread throughout New Spain into Texas.

REVOLUTION IN TEXAS

The revolutionary ideas of Father Hidalgo were accepted by his followers throughout New Spain. One such disciple, Juan Bautista de Las Casas, raised a militia force (later known as the Republican Army) and led a strike against royalists in San Antonio. On the morning of January 22, 1811, Las Casas and his rebel force seized control of San Antonio and arrested Texas governor Manuel María de Salcedo. During the time he was imprisoned, a royalist movement grew in strength. On March 2, an army of royalists freed the governor and removed Las Casas from power. He was tried for treason and executed.

Also in 1811, another follower of Hidalgo's, José Bernardo Gutiérrez de Lara, traveled to Louisiana, which had come under the control of the United States after the Louisiana Purchase in 1803. In Louisiana, Gutiérrez enlisted the help of Augustus Magee, an American military officer. Gutiérrez's force of Spanish rebels was joined by Americans to form an army of about 100 men. William Shaler, the U.S. government's representative in Louisiana, helped Gutiérrez and Magee recruit men for this invasion force.

The LOUISIANA PURCHASE

THE MISSISSIPPI RIVER WAS THE ECONOMIC LIFELINE FOR the western frontier of the newly independent United States. When Spain controlled the port of New Orleans and the lands west of the river, commerce flourished. This changed when France, through a secret treaty with Spain, regained control of the territory and closed the port of New Orleans to U.S. shipping. President Jefferson sent an envoy to Paris with orders to buy New Orleans from Napoleon, who was now dictator of France. Luckily for the United States, Napoleon's need for money to wage war against Britain outweighed his desire to re-establish an empire in North America. Napoleon offered to sell not just New Orleans but all of Louisiana. The deal was signed on May 2, 1803. For the sum of $15 million the United States gained most of the land between the Mississippi River and the Rocky Mountains, doubling the size of the country. In time, all or parts of 15 states would be created from the Louisiana Purchase.

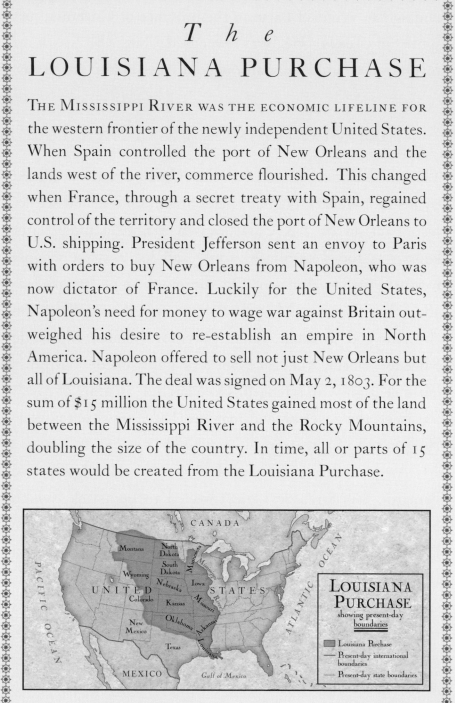

LOUISIANA PURCHASE
showing present-day boundaries

■ Louisiana Purchase
— Present-day international boundaries
⋯ Present-day state boundaries

Calling themselves the Republican Army of the North, the Gutiérrez-Magee volunteers struck first at Nacogdoches in 1811, which fell easily to the surprise attack. Word of the victory reached Louisiana, causing more volunteers to join up. *"The business of volunteering for New Spain has become a perfect mania,"* William Shaler wrote to his superiors in Washington. By the time the Gutiérrez-Magee army reached La Bahía, it had grown to 300. It easily took the Spanish settlement and began its march to San Antonio.

Officially, the U.S. government protested the rebel invasion in order to maintain peaceful relations with Spain. Off the record, however, the United States was pleased. A liberated Texas, free from Spanish rule, would open the door to U.S. expansion into the region. In a private letter to Secretary of State James Monroe, William Shaler wrote,

> *The volunteer expedition [of Gutiérrez and Magee] . . . is growing into an irresistible torrent, that will sweep the crazy remains of the Spanish Government from the Internal Provinces [Spanish territory near Louisiana, including Texas], and open Mexico to the political influence of the U.S. and to the talents and enterprise of our citizens.*

Royalist forces met the Gutiérrez-Magee army outside of San Antonio, but the rebels soon overwhelmed them. San Antonio fell. The rebels were now in charge of the capital of Texas. In April 1813, Gutiérrez issued a declaration of independence for those he called *"the people of the Province of Texas."* He also gave himself the title of "President Protector of the State of Texas."

The victors treated those they had defeated cruelly. One of Gutiérrez's captains rounded up Governor Salcedo and his aides and slit their throats. When word of this atrocity reached Las Casas's Republican Army, many men were repulsed and deserted the army. At the same time, fighting broke out between Americans and Mexicans in the rebel army.

The Posse, a painting by Theodore Gentilz, shows rebel forces gathering to do battle in Mexico's fight for independence from Spain.

A DECLARATION *of* INDEPENDENCE

FROM 1813–23, YEARS BEFORE Texas would become an independent republic — José Bernardo Gutiérrez de Lara seized control of San Antonio and issued a declaration of independence for Texas. It read:

The bonds that kept us bound to the dominion of Spain have been severed forever. . . . In the future, all legitimate authority emanates from the people where it rightly resides. From this day until the end of time, we are free from all foreign domination.

A group of rebels, outraged by Gutiérrez's actions, exiled him and made José Alvarez de Toledo new commander of the rebel army. In August, Toledo's army faced a large royalist army commanded by General Joaquín de Arredondo. At the battle of the Medina River, south of San Antonio, Arredondo's force of about 2,000 soldiers crushed the undisciplined rebel army, which numbered about 1,400. It was one of the bloodiest battles ever fought in Texas. Fewer than 100 of the 1,400 rebels survived.

In his report to the viceroy of New Spain, Arredondo wrote of his success: *"The ever victorious and invincible arms of our Sovereign [king] . . . have gained the most complete and decisive victory over the base and perfidious [disloyal] rabble commanded by certain vile assassins ridiculously styled a general and commanders."*

SPANISH INFLUENCE

IN TEXAS TODAY, THE SPANISH LANGUAGE AND THE ROMAN Catholic religion, even among Indians, are the most obvious legacies of Spain's rule. Spanish names for rivers, creeks, cities, counties, and towns dominate Texas. The Spanish introduced cattle and ranching to the region. Spanish law, architecture, theater, and music all influenced life in Texas.

Spanish influence had profound effects on the Native Americans of Texas. Many learned to speak Spanish, dress like the Spaniards, and adopt Christianity. The Spanish were influenced by the Indians, as well. Spanish settlers wore leather moccasins and buckskin clothing. The Spanish also adopted elements of the native diet, such as maize, beans, and squash.

THE END OF SPANISH RULE

Arredondo's victory was not enough to crush the spirit of revolution in New Spain. The struggle continued, and the next few years were difficult for the settlements of Texas. Royalist armies stopped many invasions by rebel militia. Then the Spanish soldiers, in the name of defending Texas took everything of value, such as food, horses, and tools.

Eventually, the rebels won more and more battles. As they grew stronger, the royalist forces scattered. Finally, Mexican independence came in 1821. Texas passed from Spanish control and became part of the new Empire of Mexico.

Antonio Martínez, the last governor of Spanish Texas, said upon leaving that *"the king's soldiers have drained the resources of the country, and laid their hands on everything that could sustain human life. The province advances at an amazing rate toward ruin and destruction. Nacogdoches is nearly expired."* At the end of Spanish rule, there were fewer colonists living in Texas than there had been at the time of the first census in 1777, which put the population at around 3,000. The years of Spanish rule were over—yet Texas, as part of an independent Mexico, would face its greatest challenges in the years to come. ※

CHAPTER SEVEN

Anglo-American Settlers

AMERICAN STEPHEN AUSTIN receives the first empresario grants to establish American colonies in Texas. This leads to many Americans coming to the territory.

hat the discovery of gold was to California, the Colonization Act of 1825 was to Texas," said Noah Smithwick. Smithwick was a North Carolina blacksmith who, in 1827, at the age of 19, moved to Texas. He lived in a settlement of Anglo-Americans (non-Spanish speaking people of European descent). His move was part of a flood of new arrivals in Texas from the United States. The Colonization Act of 1825 freed settlers from having to pay taxes to the Mexican government for four years.

OPPOSITE: "The Fandango Dancers," by Theodore Gentilz, shows Texans in Spanish-influenced dress participating in a traditional Spanish dance. Although Spanish rule in Texas ended with Mexican independence, its influence on the people and culture of the region remained strong.

Anglo-American immigration to Texas actually began in 1820, one year before Mexican independence. By that time, there were just three settlements in the area: Nacogdoches, San Antonio, and La Bahía. Spain invited Anglo-American settlers to Texas, hoping to spur economic development in the struggling region. The Spanish also hoped that additional colonies would keep the aggressive Comanche from moving into Texas from the Great Plains regions of what are now Kansas and Colorado. When Mexico achieved independence, the government continued the policy of encouraging American settlers to come to Texas.

American settlers traveling west to Texas faced a difficult journey. This engraving shows emigrants crossing Arkansas during a snowy winter.

American settlers were drawn to Texas by the lure of cheap land. In the early 1820s, undeveloped land in the United States cost $1.25 per acre. Buyers were required to purchase a minimum of 80 acres (32 ha) for a total cost of $100 and to pay the full amount in cash at the time of purchase. Land in Texas, on the other hand, sold for about four cents per acre. The standard parcel consisted of about 4,600 acres (1,860 ha), for a total cost of $184, which was payable over a period of six years.

Many Americans hoped to use this cheap land in Texas to grow cotton and then sell it to markets in the United States. The next 10 years would bring a flood of thousands of Americans into Texas.

Austin's Idea

"I have made a visit to St. [San] Antonio and obtained liberty to settle in that country—as I am ruined in this [United States], I found nothing I could do would bring back my property again and to remain in the country where I had enjoyed wealth, now in a state of poverty I could not submit to."

So wrote Moses Austin to his son, Stephen, in 1820. Moses was the first person to receive permission to bring American settlers into Texas. Stephen, who ended up carrying out his father's plan, became a key figure in the history of the state.

Moses Austin had made a fortune in the lead industry in Missouri, but by 1819, he had fallen into financial ruin during a national economic downturn. Austin traveled to San Antonio the following year, where he met with Antonio Martínez, governor of Spanish Texas. There, Austin presented his plan to bring 300 American families into Texas to settle a new colony. He spoke of the king of Spain's desire to see Texas prosper and wrote in his proposal, *"I am the agent of three hundred families who, with the same purpose in view, are desirous of seeing the intention of his Majesty fulfilled."*

Governor Martínez accepted the plan. The governor then forwarded the proposal to officials in Mexico City for approval. Meanwhile, Austin's trip back home to Missouri was a nightmare. Four weeks of traveling in the cold and rain brought on pneumonia. His food ran out, and he survived on roots and berries during the last week of his journey. Deathly ill upon reaching home, he received news that permission had been granted for him to settle the new colony in Texas.

Thrilled by his accomplishment, Austin neglected his health and worked steadily to make his dream a reality. He would never recover from his illness. In 1821, Moses Austin called his wife, Maria, to his deathbed and told her his final wish. His wish was conveyed to their son Stephen in a letter from Maria. *"'Tell dear Stephen, that it is his dying father's last request to prosecute the enterprise that he had commenced.'"* Two days later, Moses Austin was dead.

PROFILE

Stephen Austin

Stephen Austin was born on November 3, 1793, in Virginia. At the age of five, Austin moved with his family to Missouri, where his father, Moses, started a lead mining business. When Stephen was 10, his father sent him away to school in Connecticut. From there, he went to college in Kentucky before coming back to Missouri to help in his father's business. After Moses' financial ruin in 1819, Stephen helped raise funds to launch his father's Texas colonization plan. Though he wasn't excited about the plan, Stephen would become the one to see it carried out following Moses Austin's death.

AMERICAN COLONISTS

In 1821, Stephen Austin led the first group of settlers across the Sabine River, separating Louisiana from Texas. He was soon caught up in the politics of Mexican independence.

As the settlers started planting corn in Texas, Austin hurried to Mexico City, where he spent all of 1822 and part of 1823 convincing the Mexican government to honor the land grant Spain had given to his father. His success marked the beginning of the empresario system in Texas. Under this system, a man of resources like Austin, known as the *empresario*, would help bring colonists to settle on certain parcels of land. The boundaries of these parcels were set out by the Mexican government. The empresario then registered the parcels with the Mexican government in the settlers' names. This made the settlers the owners of their pieces of land.

empresario system— a system in which men of power and resources helped bring colonists to Texas to settle on land the wealthy had been given by the Mexican government

Austin's success in Mexico City led to the establishment of his first colony of 300 families between the Brazos and Colorado Rivers. In 1825, he received a second land grant from the government of Coahuila and Texas. (These two former provinces had been combined into a single Mexican state in 1824.) This time, Austin brought 500 families into the region. Between 1827 and 1831, Austin received three more grants, enabling him to bring another 1,200 families into Texas.

During 300 years of Spanish control, the population of Texas had reached a total of about 4,000. Ten years after Mexican independence, thanks to the efforts of Stephen Austin and other empresarios, the population had grown close to 20,000. Austin wrote in 1829, "*My ambition has been to succeed in redeeming Texas from its wilderness state . . . I think that I derived more satisfaction from the view of flourishing farms springing up in this wilderness than military or political chieftains do from the retrospect of their victorious campaigns.*"

EMPRESARIOS

When American colonists arrived in Texas, they were thrilled by the rich land and mild climate they found. The land between the Brazos and Colorado Rivers was lush and fertile, and the newcomers wasted no time tilling the soil and planting their crops.

Some empresarios, however, exaggerated in their advertisements to attract settlers. Sterling C. Robertson, who obtained a land grant in 1826, attracted North Carolina settler Noah Smithwick with his vision of Texas. Smithwick described what was promised:

> *Each farmer was promised 177 acres [72 ha] of irrigable farming land. . . . The woods abounded in trees, wild grapes, plums, cherries, and persimmons. . . . The climate was so mild that houses were not essential; neither was a superabundance of clothing or bedding. Corn was to be had for the planting. Mexican soldiers were stationed on the frontier to keep the Indians in check.*

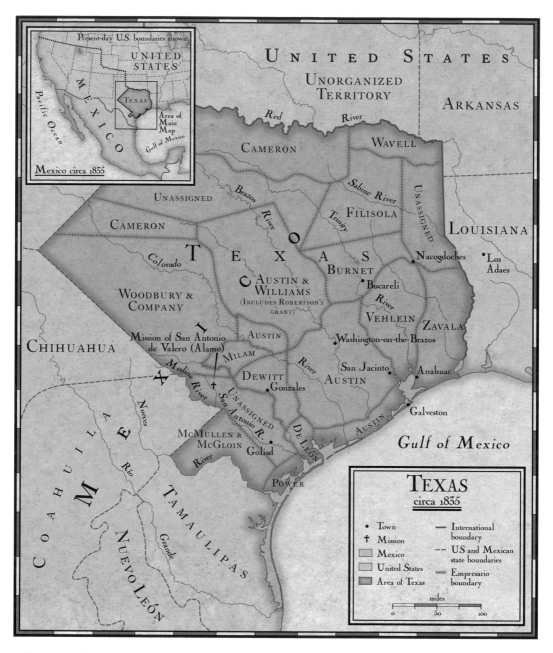

Inset map labels:
Present-day U.S. boundaries shown
UNITED STATES
MEXICO
Pacific Ocean
TEXAS
Area of Main Map
Gulf of Mexico
Mexico circa 1835

Main map labels:
UNITED STATES
UNORGANIZED TERRITORY
ARKANSAS
Red River
River
CAMERON
WAVELL
Sabine River
UNASSIGNED
FILISOLA
Trinity
LOUISIANA
UNASSIGNED
CAMERON
Brazos River
T E X A S
Nacogdoches
Los Adaes
Colorado
BURNET
AUSTIN & WILLIAMS (INCLUDES ROBERTSON'S GRANT)
Bucareli
WOODBURY & COMPANY
River
VEHLEIN
ZAVALA
CHIHUAHUA
Mission of San Antonio de Valero (Alamo)
AUSTIN
Washington-on-the-Brazos
MILAM
River
San Jacinto
Anahuac
Medina River
DEWITT
AUSTIN
C O A H U I L A
San Antonio R.
Gonzales
UNASSIGNED
Galveston
M E X I C O
Nueces
McMULLEN & McGLOIN
DE LEÓN
AUSTIN
Gulf of Mexico
TAMAULIPAS
River
Goliad
POWER
Río
NUEVO LEÓN
Grande

Legend:
TEXAS
circa 1835
• Town
✝ Mission
▢ Mexico
▢ United States
▢ Area of Texas
— International boundary
-- US and Mexican state boundaries
···· Empresario boundary
miles
0   50   100

This map shows Texas, circa 1835, when it was part of the State of Coahuila and Texas in the Republic of Mexico (see inset map). Dotted lines indicate the boundaries of individual empresarios named for the landholders who were granted territory by the Mexican government. The empresario system was designed to encourage colonization in Texas. Between 1821 and 1831 Stephen Austin brought some 2,000 American families to settle on his lands. By 1835 most Texans were thinking seriously about independence.

However, when Smithwick arrived in Texas, he found that Robertson had left out a few details. Smithwick described them as *"the hardships and privations [including drought], the ever increasing danger from the growing dissatisfaction of the Indians, upon whose hunting grounds the whites were steadily encroaching, and the almost certainty of an ultimate war with Mexico."*

Austin was more straightforward with his enticements. He wanted to assure potential settlers that no criminals would be allowed in his new colony. He replied to one prospective colonist's letter, *"No one will be . . . permitted to remain in the Province who does not bring the most unequivocal [lacking any doubt] evidence from the highest authority and most respectable men of the state and neighborhood, that he is a moral and industrious man."*

Austin's colony was laid out as a grid, or framework of streets intersecting one another, similar in fashion to traditional Mexican towns. The houses were mostly rough log cabins similar to those found in American colonies on the frontier. Among the homes were stores, inns, taverns, a government building, and a church.

SLAVERY

The Mexican government had strong feelings against slavery, yet many Americans assumed they could bring their slaves with them to Texas. Slavery had not been mentioned in Moses Austin's original request for a land grant. In the final agreement given to Stephen Austin by Mexico, slavery was allowed under the condition that in Mexico (including Texas), the children born of slaves would be free.

CRUEL MASTER

SLAVES IN THE ANGLO-AMERICAN SETTLEMENTS, WHICH were exempt from Mexico's law banning slavery, were still subject to the whims of their masters. Noah Smithwick witnessed one such incident:

Jim, one of McNeal's slaves, openly announced his determination to leave, and, acting on the impulse, threw down his hoe and started away. McNeal . . . ordered him to return to work, but Jim went on, whereupon McNeal raised his rifle.

"Jim," said he, "if you don't come back I'll shoot you!" Jim, however, kept on, and true to his threat, McNeal shot him dead.

In 1824, Mexican law placed limits on slavery. One prospective settler wrote to Austin early in 1825: *"Nothing appears at present to prevent a portion of our wealthy planters from emigrating immediately to the province of Texas but the uncertainty now prevailing with regard to slavery."* Austin dealt with this problem by recommending that settlers from the Northern, non-slave states be encouraged to move to Texas. Although the number of Northern settlers did increase somewhat, the majority of those moving to Texas still came from the nearby Southern states. Three years later, the importation of slaves into Mexico was forbidden, and in 1829, the Mexican government freed all slaves in Mexico. Texas was exempted from this decree, and the issue of slavery became a growing conflict that would divide the United States in the future.

GROWING CONFLICTS

Mexicans were disturbed by the sheer numbers of Americans pouring into Texas. A Mexican general named Manuel de Mier y Terán, who journeyed from La Bahía to Nacogdoches, wrote in 1828, *"Mexican influence is diminished. Arriving in this place [Nacogdoches] it is almost nothing. The ratio of Mexicans to foreigners is one to ten."* Luis de Onís, the Spanish minister to the United States, reflected the view of many Mexicans about their new American neighbors: *"The Americans are a litigious, over-reaching people who are continually destroying each other by horrible frauds and impositions in their transactions and dealings. . . . They think themselves superior to all the nations of Europe."*

The education of children was a point of conflict between the established residents of the former Spanish settlements in Texas and Austin's new arrivals. The 1824 constitution of the

Republic of Mexico gave responsibility for education to the states. The Constitution of Coahuila and Texas called for the establishment of primary schools in the state, but provided no way to fund the schools. By 1830, only one public school had opened, in Nacogdoches, and the Mexican attempt at public education had failed.

constitution—the written set of guiding laws and principles for a government, state, or society

The wealthiest people in the American settlements in Texas sent their children back to the United States for schooling. Under Austin's leadership, private schools opened in Texas, allowing the children of those colonists who could afford to attend these schools. The failure of the Mexican government to create a public school system ended up being listed in the Texas Declaration of Independence in 1836 as a reason for Texas to break away from Mexican rule.

Meanwhile, daily life in the American settlements went on. Shopkeepers like Noah Smithwick, the blacksmith, provided services or sold their wares. Smithwick kept a journal of his life in Texas. He wrote of a regular customer who invited Smithwick to his home for dinner:

Thomas B. Bell came several times to my shop, and . . . I gladly accepted an invitation to visit him. . . . His wife, every inch a lady, welcomed me with as much cordiality as if she were mistress of a mansion. . . . The whole family were dressed in buckskin, and when supper was announced, we sat on stools around a clapboard table, upon which were arranged wooden

platters. Beside each platter lay a fork made of cane [a bamboo-
like plant]. The knives were of various patterns, ranging from
butcher knives to pocket-knives. And for cups, we had little
wild cymlings [a type of squash], scraped and scoured until they
looked as white and clean as earthenware.

Conflicts between American colonists, Mexican
colonists, and the Mexican government over issues such as
education and slavery continued to grow. As the number of
Americans in Texas increased, they began to think of the
land as theirs. The conflicts, coupled with the Americans'
attitude, would soon lead to another revolution. ※

This 1840 lithograph shows the city of Austin, named the capital of the
Republic of Texas in 1839.

CHAPTER EIGHT

The Texas Republic and Statehood

TEXAS BREAKS AWAY FROM MEXICO. *It remains independent for nine years*, *then becomes a state in the United States.*

ature tells them [the Americans] that the land is theirs," wrote General Mier y Terán to officials in Mexico City in 1829. *"These [American] colonies . . . will be the cause for the Mexican federation to lose Texas unless measures are taken soon."* The general went on to recommend changes in Texas to prevent an American takeover of the province.

OPPOSITE: A 19th-century engraving shows Mexican General Santa Anna on horseback. His foot soldiers are attempting to scale the north wall of the Alamo, while its defenders fight them off with guns and bayonets.

The following spring, new laws based on Mier y Terán's advice—known as the April 6 Laws—went into effect. The laws established new military posts in Texas that were manned with Mexican soldiers. They banned further immigration to Texas from the United States, effectively cutting off the flow of Americans into the area. Finally, they banned the importation of any additional slaves into Texas. An outraged Stephen Austin said of the April 6 Laws, *"A more impolitic [unwise] measure could not have been adopted by this government."*

The laws of April 6, 1830, came on the heels of several key events. In 1829, U.S. president Andrew Jackson had offered to buy Texas from Mexico. Concerned about the growing power of the United States, Mexico refused the offer. Also, in 1829, Spain had launched an attack on Mexico in an attempt to recapture its lost colony. The Mexicans fought back under the leadership of General Antonio López de Santa Anna. Santa Anna's victory a month later would propel him into power and make him a major figure in the coming battle for Texas independence.

SANTA ANNA'S RISE

After his victory over the Spanish invaders, Santa Anna became a national hero. In 1833, he was elected President of Mexico. During the next two years, Santa Anna introduced legislation that reduced the power of the governments of the individual states within Mexico. Specifically, he replaced the elected government of the state of Coahuila and Texas, which by that time included representatives from Texas, with a new government that was backed by the Mexican Army.

That year, Santa Anna sent troops to reinforce military outposts in the Texas towns of Anahuac and Gonzales. The sight of Mexican troops marching into Texas inflamed the residents. A militia, led by Colonel William B. Travis, drove the Mexicans out of Anahuac and then took control of the military outposts at Gonzales and San Antonio. From that point until Texas declared itself an independent republic, Anglo-Texans, Native American Texans, and Mexican-Texans all joined forces against Santa Anna.

This portrait of Colonel William Travis, leader of the Texas militia, was made in 1835, a year before he died in battle at the Alamo.

Santa Anna was furious at the success of the Texas militia. He assembled 5,000 experienced Mexican troops armed with heavy cannon and began a march north toward Texas. He hoped to overwhelm the Texas rebels.

THE BATTLE FOR THE ALAMO

News of Santa Anna's march spread across the Texas settlements. An editorial in the *Telegraph and Texas Register* newspaper on October 10, 1835, stated, *"The alarm is sounded, and the friends of the Constitution and of constitutional liberty, are called upon to rally for the defense of their families, their homes, and their possessions."*

The leaders of the rebellion, including Stephen Austin, named General Sam Houston as commander in chief of the Texas Army. Volunteers arrived daily from the United States. Frontiersmen Jim Bowie and Davy Crockett joined General Houston and Colonel Travis, offering their services to defend Texas.

After killing the 150 Texans defending the Alamo, Santa Anna and his men watched the mission burn. Although victorious on this day, Santa Anna and his troops would not be as lucky in the battle at San Jacinto.

Early in 1836, with Santa Anna on the march, Houston sent Travis and Bowie to San Antonio to defend the city. After Crockett arrived with volunteers from Tennessee, there were about 150 men to set up a defense at the old Spanish mission San Antonio de Valero. The mission was better known as the Alamo. *Alamo* was the Spanish word for a type of cottonwood tree that grew nearby. The coming battle would be the most famous in Texas history.

On February 23, Santa Anna approached the Alamo with 5,000 soldiers. The next day, he sent a message ordering the Texans inside to surrender. Travis's reply was a cannon shot fired in defiance. Twenty-four hours later Travis sent a letter to the people of Texas informing them of the approaching battle and asking for reinforcements.

Victory or Death!

"To the people of Texas and all Americans in the world." So began Colonel William B. Travis's now famous letter of February 24, 1836, the contents of which made their way throughout the Texas colonies and beyond as the battle of the Alamo began. At first, the original letter, carried from the Alamo by a captain named Albert Martin, was hand-copied and sent to many towns. Eventually, it was printed in the March 2 issue of the *Texas Republican* newspaper, and many more people got to read it. Travis wrote:

I have answered their demand for surrender with a cannon shot and our flag still waves proudly from the walls. The fort has sustained a continual bombardment and cannonade for 24 hours. . . . I shall never surrender or retreat. . . . Victory or Death!"

Santa Anna responded to the cannon shot by firing at the Alamo's walls. The assault lasted almost two weeks. By March 5, the walls of the Alamo were just about down, and very few reinforcements had arrived. Santa Anna could simply have waited out the Texans, but he ordered his troops to storm the Alamo early the next morning.

The resulting battle on March 6 left all of the Alamo's defenders dead, including Colonel Travis, along with 600 of Santa Anna's own troops. Travis and his men at the Alamo would have been proud to know that four days earlier, on March 2, the Texas Declaration of Independence had been signed by representatives at a convention in the town of Washington-on-the-Brazos. This document declared Texas to be a free and independent republic.

The TEXAS DECLARATION of INDEPENDENCE

THE TEXAS DECLARATION OF Independence listed grievances against the Mexican government, including its change from a republic to a military dictatorship and its failure to provide public education, trial by jury, and freedom of religion.

The necessity of self-preservation . . . now decrees our eternal political separation. We therefore . . . do hereby resolve and declare, that our political connection with the Mexican nation has forever ended, and that the people of Texas do now constitute a free, sovereign, and independent republic.

Although the Texans suffered a crushing defeat at the Alamo, word of the stand made by Travis and his men spread through Texas. Cries of "Remember the Alamo!" incited volunteers to join General Houston's army. Six weeks after the fall of the Alamo, Houston led a force of close to 1,000 soldiers against Santa Anna's army near the town of San Jacinto.

Despite being greatly outnumbered by Santa Anna, Houston's attack on April 21, 1836, had the element of surprise on its side. Houston's men used the hills and tall grass to conceal their approach until the moment they struck.

"The Surrender of Santa Anna," an 1886 oil painting by William Henry Huddle, shows the Mexican general (in white pants, hat in hand) conceding defeat to a wounded Sam Houston (lying against the tree) on April 22, 1836.

The Mexican troops were also extremely fatigued from a long march the previous night, and most were asleep when Houston's army attacked. The Texans defeated Santa Anna's army in what was the last battle of the Texas Revolution. The battle was over in eighteen minutes. The Mexicans sustained heavy casualties, while the Texans had very few. Santa Anna was captured the following day.

The Mexican leader described the surprise attack this way: "*I saw our men flying in small groups, terrified, and sheltering themselves behind large trees. I endeavored to force some of them to fight, but . . . they were a bewildered and panic-stricken herd.*"

General Sam Houston, commander in chief of the Texas Army and the first president of the independent Republic of Texas

LIFE IN THE TEXAS REPUBLIC

Texas was now an independent nation. War hero Sam Houston was elected the first president of Texas. Stephen Austin had very much wanted to be president, but he was beaten by Houston in the election by a nine to one margin. Instead, Austin graciously accepted the position of Houston's secretary of state.

Life in the new republic was difficult and dangerous. Much of the danger came from Comanche attacks. President Houston wanted to establish a treaty with the Comanche. He sent Noah Smithwick, a long-time resident of the region and friend of the Indians, to negotiate. "*The white people, weary of the perpetual warfare which compelled them to live in forts and make a subsistence as best they might, hailed the proposition for a treaty with delight,*" Smithwick wrote.

Smithwick spoke with Comanche leaders about the conflicting claims of the white settlers and the natives to the land in Texas. Smithwick asked a Comanche chief named Muguara how he thought the conflict could be settled. Chief Muguara replied, "*If the white men would draw a line defining their claims and keep on their side of it, the red men would not molest them.*"

Smithwick brought this idea back to Houston, who agreed that it was a good solution. However, the Texas legislature, and Texans in general, wanted no part of it. The overwhelming feeling among Texans was that the Comanche should be driven out of the territory by force, an attitude that led to many more years of conflict and bloodshed.

Meanwhile Texas was being assaulted by Mexico from the south. Despite his defeat at San Jacinto, Santa Anna never recognized Texas independence. He sent troops to San Antonio to try to retake the area. Although Texas troops drove the Mexican Army out, these attacks drained manpower and resources away from the already struggling newly independent republic.

Economic Woes

Adding to the difficulties of the new republic were the horrible economic conditions in the United States. A bank panic, in which the value of paper money dropped because there was too much of it in circulation, sent the United States into an economic depression from 1837 until 1845—basically the entire period that the Republic of Texas existed. Texas had no banks of its own during these years. Paper money from Louisiana and Mississippi was accepted in Texas, but when banks started to fail in the United States in 1837, that paper money became worthless. Texans began to barter for goods and services.

Smithwick wrote,

> . . . owing to the constant drain on . . . [the supply of horses] by the horse-loving Indians [who would steal the horses during raids], that kind of currency became scarce, so we settled on the cow as the least liable to [change in value].

Drunk and Disorderly

The constant threat of attack from Indians from the north and Mexicans from the south had another effect on life in the Republic of Texas. A large part of the population was made up of soldiers. In between skirmishes, these men sometimes had time on their hands, so they filled saloons and gambling dens. The combination of liquor and gambling often led to huge drunken brawls and general disorder. A traveler from Ohio wrote home about his experiences among Texas soldiers:

> It appeared to be the business of the great mass of people to collect around these centers of vice and hold their drunken orgies.
> . . . Some of the scenes which took place in the streets exceeded description and afforded a melancholy proof to what a point of degradation [dishonor or shame] human nature may descend.

Devout Spanish Catholics lived in the midst of a military culture that was often at odds with their work as missionaries. "The Romance of Tragedy of Pioneer Life" by Augustus L. Mason shows gamblers outside a mission, making the sign of the cross as Spanish friars pass by.

The chaos of life in the republic did not stop new settlers from coming into Texas. Land was still very cheap,
and slavery was allowed. Also, criminals and debtors from
the United States found Texas a convenient place to hide
from the law.

As a result, despite all its problems, the population of
Texas grew from 50,000 to 125,000 during the nine years
it was a republic. In time, however, the people living in
Texas began to wonder about its future. *"A general gloom seems
to rest over every section of the Republic,"* said an 1842 newspaper
editorial, *"and doubt and sorrow are depicted on almost every brow."*

STATEHOOD

In 1844, former U.S. President Andrew Jackson, now in
failing health, wrote to his former advisers, Francis Blair
and William Lewis. A longtime supporter
of annexing Texas as a U.S. state, Jackson
asked his friends to press Congress to
approve annexation. *"The annexation of Texas
is all important to the security and the future peace
and prosperity of our Union,"* he wrote.

annex—to incorporate a
region into the territory
of another state or nation

Houston agreed. Writing to Jackson, the president of
Texas declared: *"I am determined upon immediate annexation to the
United States."* Despite its growing population, Texas could
no longer stand alone. Years of attacks by Indians and
Mexico, coupled with financial hardship, had taken their

toll. Houston strongly believed that becoming part of the United States was the best plan for Texas. If the United States did not act, Mexico might once again grab Texas.

After much debate, Congress finally approved annexation. On October 13, 1845, the people of Texas overwhelmingly voted for annexation and adopted a new constitution. On December 29, President James Polk signed the Joint Resolution for the Admission of the State of Texas into the Union making Texas the 28th state.

On his deathbed, Jackson received the happy news from Blair, who said, *"I congratulate you on the success of the great question which you put in action."* Jackson replied weakly, *"I not only rejoice, but congratulate my beloved country. Texas is [annexed], and the safety, prosperity, and the greatest interest of the whole Union is secured."* The long journey of Texas from Spanish colony to a state within the United States was now complete. ❈

Time Line

1528 Álvar Núñez Cabeza de Vaca becomes the first European to set foot in the land that would one day be known as Texas.

1685 French explorer René-Robert Cavelier, Sieur de La Salle, establishes the colony of Fort St. Louis, reigniting Spanish interest in colonizing Texas.

1690 Alonso de León and Father Damián Massanet establish the mission San Francisco de los Tejas, the first permanent Spanish settlement in Texas.

1714 French soldier and explorer Louis Juchereau de Saint-Denis establishes a mission in Natchitoches, in French Louisiana, near the border with Texas, fueling even greater Spanish interest in Texas.

1718 Texas governor Martín de Alarcón and Father Antonio de San Buenaventura y Olivares establish a mission, San Antonio de Valero, and a presidio, San Antonio de Béxar. These settlements would become the city of San Antonio.

1721 The Marqués de San Miguel de Aguayo leads thousands of people, cattle, horses, sheep, and goats into Texas. He establishes new missions and presidios and introduces ranching to Texas.

1731 Canary Island settlers arrive in San Antonio.

1758 A Comanche raid on the mission at San Sabá results in the murder of eight priests and the destruction of the mission.

1772 King Carlos III of Spain issues the "New Regulations for Presidios." These orders require the abandonment of all presidios in Texas except for those at San Antonio and La Bahía. They name San Antonio as the capital of Texas and require the relocation of everyone from East Texas to San Antonio.

1783 The United States of America is born. Spain's power on the North American continent is threatened.

1785 Peace treaties with the Comanche trigger a population boom in San Antonio, as ranchers and farmers buy the cheap, plentiful land.

1810 Father Miguel Hidalgo y Costilla organizes revolutionary actions against Spanish control of Mexico. This marks the beginning of the Mexican independence movement.

1813 José Bernardo Gutiérrez de Lara seizes control of San Antonio and declares Texas an independent republic. General Joaquín de Arredondo recaptures control of San Antonio for Spain.

1821 Mexico becomes an independent nation, free from Spanish rule. American Stephen Austin receives the first empresario grant to establish American settlements in Texas.

1829 The Mexican government bans slavery. General Antonio López de Santa Anna leads the Mexican Army as it repels a Spanish attempt to take back Mexico.

1830 The Mexican government's "April 6 Laws" ban further American immigration into Texas.

1833 Santa Anna is elected president of Mexico.

1834 Santa Anna declares himself dictator of Mexico.

1835 Santa Anna replaces the government of Texas with military rulers who would report directly to him in Mexico City.

1836 The battles of the Alamo and San Jacinto are fought. Texas becomes an independent republic after Santa Anna surrenders at San Jacinto.

1845 Texas becomes the 28th state of the United States of America.

RESOURCES

BOOKS

Carey, Charles W., Jr. *The Mexican War.* Berkeley Heights, N.J.: Enslow Publishers, Inc., 2002.

Chipman, Donald E. and Joseph, Harriett Denise. *Explorers and Settlers of Spanish Texas: Men and Women of Spanish Texas.* Austin: University of Texas Press, 2001.

Littlejohn, E.G. *Texas History Stories.* Abilene, Tex: State House Press, 1987.

McComb, David G. *Texas: An Illustrated History.* Oxford: Oxford University Press, 1995.

Nardo, Don. *The Mexican-American War.* San Diego: Lucent Books, 1999.

* Reséndez, Andrés. *Changing National Identities at the Frontier: Texas and New Mexico, 1800–1850.* Cambridge University Press, 2004.

Santella, Andrew. *The Battle of the Alamo.* Danbury, Conn.: Children's Press. 1997.

* College-level sources

WEB SITES

The Library of Congress Presents America's Story from America's Library
http://www.americaslibrary.gov/cgi-bin/page.cgi
This Web page for kids from the Library of Congress contains fascinating information on Texas and other American colonies.

Texas Online—The Awesome Lone Star State
http://texas-on-line.com/graphic/history.htm
This site contains facts and figures, as well as a concise history of Texas.

Texas State Historical Association—The Handbook of Texas Online
http://www.tsha.utexas.edu/handbook/online/
This site is an online encyclopedia of Texas, featuring excellent biographies of key figures.

Texas State Library and Archives Commission
http://www.tsl.state.tx.us/
This comprehensive site has great details on all aspects of Texas history.

The University of Texas at Austin—Texas Beyond History
http://www.texasbeyondhistory.net/
This virtual museum highlights Texas's cultural heritage.

QUOTE SOURCES

INTRODUCTION

p. 10 "I could have. . . people never make it." Steinbeck, John. *Travels With Charley: In Search of America*. New York: Penguin 1962; "like most passionate. . . not limited by, facts." Steinbeck, pp. 173-175.

CHAPTER ONE

p. 16 "It seemed to me. . . better adapted to settlement." http://www.pbs.org/weta/ thewest/resources/archives/one/cabeza.htm The Journey of Alvar Nuñez Cabeza De Vaca (1542). p. 19 "Every day our thirst. . . rotten and useless." http://www.pbs.org/weta/ thewest/resources/archives/one/cabeza.htm The Journey of Alvar Nuñez Cabeza De Vaca (1542). "each must do. . . save himself." http://www.pbs.org/weta/thewest/resources/ archives/one/cabeza.htm The Journey of Alvar Nuñez Cabeza De Vaca (1542).

CHAPTER TWO

p. 22 "The ship was stranded. . . enterprize and settlement." Joutel, Henri. *A Journal of La Salle's Last Voyage*. New York: Corinth Books, 1962, p. 51; "30 casks of. . . and grain." Joutel, p. 53; "We fell to. . . the seas threw up." Joutel, p. 57; "about an hundred. . . bows and arrows." Joutel, p. 52; p. 23 "We had an. . . alligators in the rivers." Joutel, p. 52; p. 26 "We. . . found six. . . many dead pigs." Bolton, Herbert Eugene. *Spanish Exploration in the Southwest 1542-1706*. New York: Charles Scribner's Sons, 1916, p. 362; p. 27 "Five Indians had come. . . could not carry it off." Bolton, p. 403.

CHAPTER THREE

p. 30 "The Indians lived. . . grinding corn into meal." Bolton, Herbert Eugene. *Spanish Exploration in the Southwest 1542-1706*. New York: Charles Scribner's Sons, 1916, p. 378; p. 31 "We found a delightful. . . dwelling and a church." Bolton, p. 380; p.32 "Seeing that all. . . occurred to me." Weber, David J. *The Spanish Frontier in North America*. New Haven and London: Yale University Press, 1992, p. 160; p. 34 "could supply. . . but a city." Weber, p. 163; p. 35 "The settlers early. . . beans, and vegetables." De la Teja, Jesús F. *San Antonio de Béxar: A Community on Spain's Northern Frontier*. Albuquerque: University of New Mexico Press, 1995; p. 37 "This presidio is. . . perform their duty." De la Teja; "It must be recognized. . . New Spain." De la Teja.

CHAPTER FOUR

p. 42 "we found nails. . . by the French." Weber, David J. *The Spanish Frontier in North America*. New Haven and London: Yale University Press, 1992, p. 168; p.43 "The fourteen families. . . entire province." De la Teja, Jesús F. *San Antonio de Béxar: A Community on Spain's Northern Frontier*. Albuquerque: University of New Mexico Press, 1995.

CHAPTER FIVE

p. 50 "Indians had been. . . squash and maize." De la Teja, Jesús F. *San Antonio de Béxar: A Community on Spain's Northern Frontier*. Albuquerque: University of New Mexico Press, 1995, p. 46; pp.51-52 "neither force a. . . are really ill." Faulk, Odie B. *The Last Years of Spanish Texas 1778-1821*. London, The Hague, Paris: Mouton & Co., 1964, p. 76; p. 55 "Bexar Presidential Report—October 1778." Faulk, p. 51; p. 56 "I wish to procure. . . are sufficient." Faulk, p. 103; p. 59 "with rare exceptions. . . and corruptly managed." Chipman, Donald E. *Spanish Texas 1519-1821*. Austin: The University of Texas Press, 1992, p. 180.

CHAPTER SIX

p. 66 "From the moment. . . fortune from progressing." Hamill, Jr., Hugh M. *The Hidalgo Revolt: Prelude to Mexican Independence*. Gainesville: University of Florida Press, 1966, p. 195; "To arms,. . . banners that you abhor." Hamill, Jr., p. 193; p. 71 "The business. . . perfect mania." Brands, H.W. *Lone Star Nation*. New York, Toronto, London, Auckland, Sydney: Doubleday, 2004, p. 39; "The volunteer expedition. . . enterprise of our citizens." Brands, p. 40; pp. 71-72 "the people of. . . Texas. Brands, p. 40; p. 73 "The ever victorious. . . general and commanders." Chipman, Donald E. *Spanish Texas 1519-1821*. Austin: The University of Texas Press, 1992, p. 237; p. 75 "the king's soldiers. . . is nearly expired." Chipman, p. 240.

CHAPTER SEVEN

p. 77 "What the discovery. . . was to Texas." Smithwick, Noah. *The Evolution of a State or Recollections of Old Texas Days*. Austin: The University of Texas Press, 1983, p. 1; p. 79 "I have made. . . I could not submit to." Cantrell, Gregg. *Stephen F. Austin, Empresario of Texas*. New Haven and London: Yale University Press, 1999; p. 80 "I am the agent

. . . his Majesty fulfilled." Brands, H.W. *Lone Star Nation*. New York, Toronto, London, Auckland, Sydney: Doubleday, 2004, p. 22; "Tell dear Stephen. . . he had commenced." Brands, p.24; p. 83 "My ambition has. . . their victorious campaigns." Cantrell, p. 1; "Each farmer was. . . Indians in check." Smithwick, p. 1; p. 85 "the hardships and. . . war with Mexico." Smithwick, p. 1; "No one will be. . . moral and industrious man." Lowrie, Samuel Harman. *Culture Conflict in Texas 1821-1835*. New York: Columbia University, 1932, p. 42; pp. 86-87 "Nothing appears at. . . regard to slavery." Lowrie, p. 49; p. 87 "Mexican influence is. . . one to ten." Lowrie, p. 82; "The Americans are. . . nations of Europe." Lowrie, p. 95; pp. 88-89 "Thomas B. Bell. . . clean as earthenware." Smithwick, p. 24.

CHAPTER EIGHT

p.91 "Nature tells them. . . land is theirs." Brands, H.W. *Lone Star Nation*. New York, Toronto, London, Auckland, Sydney: Doubleday, 2004, p. 151; "These [American] colonies. . . are taken soon." Brands, p. 151; p. 92 "A more impolitic. . . by this government." Brands, p.156; p. 94 "The alarm is sounded. . . and their possessions." Clark, Carol Lea. *Imagining Texas: Pre-Revolutionary Texas Newspapers 1829-1836*. El Paso: University of Texas at El Paso, 2003, p. 21; p. 95 "I have answered their. . . Victory or Death!" Santella, Andrew. *The Battle of the Alamo*. Danbury: Children's Press, 1997, p. 20; p. 96 "The necessity of. . . independent republic." http://www.lsjunction.com/docs/ tdoi.htm. p.98 "I saw our men. . . panic-stricken herd." Brands, p. 451; p. 99 "The white people. . . treaty with delight." Brands, p. 488; "If the white men. . . not molest them." Brands, p. 490; ". . . But owing to. . . [change in value]." Brands, p. 494; p. 101 "It appeared to. . . nature may descend." Brands, p. 497; p. 102 "A general gloom. . . almost every brow." Brands, p. 499; "The annexation of. . . of our Union." Brands, p. 503; "I am determined. . . the United States." Brands, p. 503; p. 103 "I congratulate you. . . Union is secured." Brands, pp. 507-508.

INDEX

ABOUT THE AUTHOR

MICHAEL TEITELBAUM has been a writer and editor of children's books and magazines for more than 25 years. His nonfiction work includes books on the Colonies, the U.S. Constitution, and sports in America. He was also the editor of *Little League Magazine* for children and the author of a two-volume encyclopedia on the Baseball Hall of Fame. He and his wife split their time between New York City and their 170-year-old farmhouse in upstate New York.

ANDRÉS RESÉNDEZ is an assistant professor of history at the University of California at Davis. He earned his Ph.D. in history from the University of Chicago. A native of Mexico, Reséndez has written numerous books and articles on Spanish Texas and the history of the state's border disputes with Mexico. He lives in Davis, California.

ILLUSTRATION CREDITS

Cover, pages 35, 48, 52, 67:
University of Texas Institute of Texan Culture at San Antonio

Title Page, page 38:
The Center for American History, The University of Texas at Austin

Pages 8, 10, 81, 93, 97:
Texas State Library and Archives Commission

Pages 9, 12, 14, 28, 57, 64, 78, 89, 90, 98:
The Granger Collection

Page 17:
American Antiquarian Society

Pages 18, 45, 70, 89:
National Geographic Society

Pages 20, 41, 47, 61:
Picture Collection, The Branch Libraries, The New York Public Library

Page 24:
The Getty Collection

Pages 36 (detail of original):
Art Resource

Pages 72, 76, 101:
Bridgeman Art Library

Page 94:
North Wind Picture Archives

End sheets, page 51:
The Library of Congress

NORTH AMERICA Divided into its III PRINCIPALL PARTS 1e ENGLISH Part viz ENGLISH EMPIRE co

N Foundland N Scotland N England N York N Jarsey Pensylvania Maryland Virginia Carolina Carolania or Florida California Sommer Is Bahama Is Jamaica &c. CARIBY I. II SPANISH I

1685

BAFFI
BAY

ARCTI

NEW NORTH
WALES

NEW SOUTH
WALES

SEA OF CALIFORNIA

NEW ALBION

NEW MEXICO

Tract of Land
full of Wild Bulls

LAKE SUPERIOR

NEW MEXICO

MARA

NEW BISCAIA

ZACATECAS

THE GOLF OR
BAY OF
MEXICO

SEA

OF

NEW SPAIN

YUCATAN